The PATRICIA LYNN ★PROJECT★

The PATRICIA LYNN PROJECT

VIETNAM WAR, THE EARLY YEARS OF AIR INTELLIGENCE

DAVID KARMES

THE PATRICIA LYNN PROJECT
VIETNAM WAR, THE EARLY YEARS OF AIR INTELLIGENCE

Copyright © 2014 David Karmes.

All rights reserved. No part of this book may be used or reproduced by any means, graphic, electronic, or mechanical, including photocopying, recording, taping or by any information storage retrieval system without the written permission of the publisher except in the case of brief quotations embodied in critical articles and reviews.

iUniverse books may be ordered through booksellers or by contacting:

iUniverse
1663 Liberty Drive
Bloomington, IN 47403
www.iuniverse.com
1-800-Authors (1-800-288-4677)

Because of the dynamic nature of the Internet, any web addresses or links contained in this book may have changed since publication and may no longer be valid. The views expressed in this work are solely those of the author and do not necessarily reflect the views of the publisher, and the publisher hereby disclaims any responsibility for them.

Any people depicted in stock imagery provided by Thinkstock are models, and such images are being used for illustrative purposes only.
Certain stock imagery © Thinkstock.

ISBN: 978-1-4917-5227-2 (sc)
ISBN: 978-1-4917-5228-9 (e)

Library of Congress Control Number: 2014920655

Printed in the United States of America.

iUniverse rev. date: 12/03/2014

CONTENTS

Preface ix
    The Vietnam Memorial Wall in Washington D.C. ix

Introduction xiii
    Why Were We in Vietnam xiii
    The Orders xv

Chapter 1:   June 1964 1
    The Trip Over 1
    Tan Son Nhut Airbase 9
    The Awesome B-57 Aircraft 13
    My first trip to Saigon 21
    Trip to Vung Tau 25

Chapter 2:   July 1964 28
    First Firefight 28
    Sky Rader Crash 29
    Party Time 33

Chapter 3:   August 1964 38
    The War Begins 38
    Chinese Jets in North Vietnam 42
    Ninety Six Huey Helicopters 45
    Our night off 47
    Jet Fighter Races 48

Chapter 4: September 1964 54
    Student Unrest 54
    Coup d'état 59
    General Nguyen Cao Ky 62

Chapter 5: October 1964 65
    Mohawk Crash 65
    243sClose Call 68

Chapter 6: November 1964 70
    Bien Hoe Mortar Attack 70
    I get to fly in my aircraft 74
    Bombed in Saigon 75

Chapter 7: December 1964 77
    F100 Crash 77
    New Aircraft (237) Arrives 79
    Bob Hope Sneaks into Vietnam 79

Chapter 8: January 1965 84
    New Weird Bomb 85
    First Combat Mission for My new Aircraft 88
    Sand bag Revetments 91

Chapter 9: Febuary 1965 93
    Burn Down the Black Forest 93
    C-47 Cargo Aircraft Crash 95
    The first attack on North Vietnam by South Vietnam. 96
    Spooky Dudes Show up 101
    F-102 Crash (My Big Mistake) 102
    More Chinese Jets 105
    Another Coup 106

Chapter 10: March 1965 112
  U. S. Jets in combat for the first time in South Vietnam 112
  Big Snake 114
  F-4C Phantom Jets Arrive in South East Asia 115
  237 in Trouble 115
  The Lazy Dog Bomb 116
  United States Embassy Bombed 122

Chapter 11: April 1965 124
  Major Musgrove's 100th Combat mission 124
  Viet Cong after ME 127
  More Jets Sent to Vietnam 128
  Largest Air Operation of the war to date 129
  Huge firefight 132

Chapter 12: May 1965 134
  245 Returns from General Dynamics 134
  Puff the Magic Dragon 136
  245 a very Special Aircraft 138
  Russian Surface to Air Missile sites (SAM) 140
  Disaster at Bien Hoa Airbase 141
  Armed B-57Bs Arrive at Ton Son Nhut 144
  Going Home 145

PREFACE

For many years I have wanted to write a book about my experience in Vietnam in 1964 and 1965 in the United States Air Force as a jet fighter mechanic. My wife, Sheila, and I were prolific letter writers during the year I was away in Vietnam. Sheila saved all the letters I wrote to her over 50 years ago in 3 shoeboxes. In those letters were many personal things I wrote to her, but also everything that was happening to me and around me. We will concentrate on what I was experiencing.

I laid out all the letters and separated them by month then by post marked date. Then I purchased an account with Stars & Stripes Newspaper archives where I could go back and search the paper by date to get more information.

You don't hear much about the Vietnam Vets that were not directly in combat, although we were in constant danger, as there were no behind the lines in Vietnam. Over 58,000 of my brothers and sisters were killed in that war. I always felt bad that I made it out of there without a scratch. But as I researched for this book I came to realize those I worked with and I were responsible for saving hundreds, maybe thousands of our troops, and our Allies troops. We used some very secret and very special reconnaissance aircraft that we could see directly into the jungle with. I will explain the airplane later in detail plus my personal experiences in the year I was in Vietnam.

The Vietnam Memorial Wall in Washington D.C.

This is interesting Veterans Statistics from the Vietnam Memorial wall that was sent to me by my brother in-law. The author is unknown; probably someone in the U.S. Government compiled it. I have added some of my own words also.

I think the Vietnam Memorial wall is something this country got right. Here is A little history most people will never know.

There are 58,267 names now listed on that polished black wall, including those added in 2010. The names are arranged in the order in which they were taken from us by date and within each date the names are alphabetized. It is hard to believe it is over 40 years since the last casualties.

The first known casualty was Richard B. Fitzgibbon, of North Weymouth, Mass. listed by the US Department of Defense as having been killed on June 8, 1956. His name is listed on the wall with that of his son, Marine Corps Lance Cpl, Richard B. Fitzgibbon III who was killed on September 7, 1965. There are three sets of fathers and sons on the wall. There are 31 sets of brothers on the wall. Thirty one sets of parents lost two of their sons.

On the wall 39,996 soldiers were just 22 years old or younger. There were 8,283 just 19 years old. The largest age group, 33,103 were 18 years old. There were 12 soldiers on the wall just 17 years old. Five soldiers on the wall were 16 years old. One soldier Pfc. Dan Bullock was 15 years old. There were 997 soldiers killed on their first day in Vietnam. Plus 1,448 soldiers were killed on their last day in Vietnam. Eight women are on the wall, they were nursing the wounded. There were 244 soldiers awarded the Medal of Honor during the Vietnam War, 153 of them are on the wall.

West Virginia had the highest casualty rate per capita in the nation. There are 711 W. Virginians on the wall. Beallsville, Ohio with a population of 475 lost six of her sons. In the little copper mining town of Morenci Arizona, population 5,058, nine graduates of Morenci High enlisted as a group in the Marine Corps. Their service began on Independence Day, 1966 and only three returned home. The most casualty deaths for a single day was on January 31, 1968, 245of our brave soldiers died. The most casualty deaths for a single month was May 1968 2,415 casualties were incurred.

For most of you who read these Statistics you will only see the numbers that the Vietnam War created. To those of us who survived the war, and to the families of those who did not, we see the faces, we feel the pain that these numbers created. We are, until we too pass away, haunted with these numbers, because they were our friends, fathers, husbands, wives, sons and daughters. THERE ARE NO NOBLE WARS, JUST NOBLE WARRIORS.

INTRODUCTION

Why Were We in Vietnam

Here is a partial text of a United States white paper on Vietnam compiled in early 1965. It may help explain why we were there.

From the U.S. State Dept- South Vietnam is fighting for its life against a brutal campaign of terror and armed attack inspired, directed, supplied and controlled by the communist regime in North Vietnam. This flagrant aggression has been going on for years, but recently the pace has quickened and the threat has now become acute. The war in Vietnam is a new kind of war, a fact as yet poorly understood in most parts of the world. Much of the confusion that prevails in the thinking of many people and even many governments stems from this basic misunderstanding. For in Vietnam a totally new brand of aggression has been loosed against an independent people who want to make their own way in peace and freedom. In Vietnam the communist government in the north has set out deliberately to conquer a sovereign people in a neighboring state, and to achieve its end it has used every resource of its own government to carry out its carefully planned program of concealed aggression. North Vietnam's commitment to seize control of the south is just as total as was the commitment of the regime in North Korea in 1950 to conquer South Korea. But knowing the consequences of the latter's undisguised attack; the planners in Hanoi have tried desperately to conceal their hand. They have failed and their aggression is as real as that of an invading army.

This report is a summary of the massive evidence of the North Vietnamese aggression obtained by the government of South Vietnam. This evidence has been jointly analyzed by South Vietnamese and American experts. The evidence shows that the hard-core of the communist forces attacking South Vietnam were trained in the north and ordered into the south by Hanoi. It shows that the key leadership of the Viet Cong, the officers and much of the cadre, many of the technicians, political organizers and propagandists come from the North and operate under Hanoi's direction. It shows that the training of essential military personnel and their infiltration into the south is directed by the military high command in Hanoi. The evidence shows that many of the weapons and much of the ammunition and other supplies used by the Viet Cong have been sent into South Vietnam from Hanoi. In recent months new types of weapons have been introduced into the Viet Cong Army for which all ammunition must come from outside sources. Communist China and other communist states have been the prime suppliers of these weapons and ammunition and they have primarily channeled through North Vietnam. Hanoi supplies the key personnel for the armed aggression against South Vietnam. The hard core of communist forces attacking South Vietnam are men trained in North Vietnam and they are ordered into the south and remain under the military discipline of the military command in Hanoi.

Special training camps operated by the North Vietnamese Army give political and military training to the infiltrators. Increasingly the forces that entered the South are native North Vietnamese who have never seen South Vietnam. The infiltration rate has been increasing, from 1959 to 1960 when Hanoi was establishing its infiltration pipeline, at least 1800 men and probably 2700 more moved into South Vietnam from the North. The flow increased to a minimum of 3700 in 1961 and at least 5400 in 1962. In 1963 there were 4200, for this year in 1964 the evidence is still incomplete. However it already shows that a minimum of 1400 infiltrators entered the South and more than 3000 others probably were sent in. There is usually a time lag between the entry of infiltrating troops and the discovery of clear evidence they have entered. This fact plus collateral evidence of increased use of the infiltration routes suggest strongly that 1964 is probably the year of the greatest infiltration so far.

Thus since 1959 nearly 20,000 Viet Cong officers, soldiers and technicians are known to have entered South Vietnam under orders from Hanoi. It is now estimated the Viet Cong number approximately 35,000 so-called hard core forces and another 60,000 to 80,000 local forces. It is thus apparent that infiltrators from the North make up the majority and probably the overwhelming portion of the so-called hard-core Viet Cong. Personnel from the North in short, are now and have always been the backbone of the entire Viet Cong operation. The heart of the Viet Cong intelligence organization is the Central Research Bureau in Hanoi. Communist agents are regularly dispatched from North Vietnam, sometimes for brief assignments but often for long periods. Many of these agents moved into South Vietnam along the infiltration trails through Laos. But others are carried by boats along the coast and landed at prearranged sites. A special maritime infiltration group has been developed in North Vietnam and its operations are centered in Ha Tinh and Quang Binh provinces just north of the 17th parallel. Today the war in Vietnam has reached new levels of intensity. The elaborate effort by the communist regime in North Vietnam to conquer the South has grown, not diminished. Military men, technicians, political organizers, propagandists and secret agents have been infiltrating the Republic of South Vietnam from the north in growing numbers. The government in Saigon has undertaken vigorous action to meet the new threats. The United States and other free countries have increased their assistance to the Vietnamese government and people.

This is the reason I, and many others, were sent to South Vietnam to help protect them from the North Vietnamese communist.

The Orders

I joined the U.S. Air Force on July 9, 1961 right after I graduated from high school in Delton Michigan, and was trained as a Jet Fighter Mechanic 1 & 2 engines. My first duty station was at McConnell AFB, Wichita, Kansas where I met and married my beautiful wife, Sheila. In 1963 we were transferred to Turner AFB, Albany, Georgia where we were expecting to remain until my enlistment was up in 1965. We had just recently purchased a house trailer and had a nice lot just off base and were considering starting a family.

Then come the orders. In April of 1964, I was working in base flight as a jet fighter mechanic, although we had no jet fighters. We did have two T-33 single engine jet trainers and 30 B-52 bombers and a dozen KC-135 refueling tankers.

I was working 2nd shift in transit alert taking care of aircraft just passing through. We were also charged with picking up B-52 drag chutes. We would take turns going out to pick up the B-52 drag chutes, and usually the boss would go unless he had other things to do. The reason he would go was that it was absolutely awesome to watch the B-52's land. We would back the truck up just off the end of the runway so we could see straight down the runway. Probably one of the most awesome sights you will ever see is to watch a B-52 land in a cross wind. The nose of the aircraft would be hanging over the grass on the right side of the runway and the tail over the grass on the other side. The B-52 has crosswind landing gear so the pilot could turn the wheels to go straight down the runway no matter which way the airplane is pointing. Then when the airplane was firmly on the ground they would slowly turn the airplane to point straight, then pop the drag chute and hit the brakes.

My boss and I were out hooking drag chutes on the back of our (Follow Me) pickup truck after the bombers landed and dragging them down the taxiway to remove the rattlesnakes. In the winter time in southern Georgia the snakes would come up out of the river that runs around the end of the runway to get warm on the concrete ramp. It was very dangerous work and rarely did we not have one or two tangled up in the chute. We received a call on the radio from dispatch that I had new orders that had just come in and to pick them up at the office. We packed the drag chutes in the back of the truck and headed up to the office. I had wanted to be transferred from Turner AFB in Albany Georgia as Sheila, my wife, and I did not like the hot humid summers of southern Georgia.

I was not ready for the orders I received, (Vietnam). I was to report to Travis Air Force Base in San Francisco, California on June 7, 1964, for transportation to the 405th Fighter Wing, Clark AFB, in the Philippines, then to Detachment I, 33rd Tactical Group Tan Son Nhut Airbase, at Saigon, South Vietnam. I was surprised because I had just seen on the news that we had NO Jets stationed in Vietnam. Although when I arrived there in June, there were many jets. I will elaborate on that later.

We sold our trailer and packed everything we owned in our 1960 Ford Star liner. (Wish I still had that car.) We headed for Michigan for a week where I grew up, to visit my parents and family. We then went to Derby,

Kansas where Sheila's folks lived and where she was going stay while I was in Vietnam. Derby is close to McConnell AFB where she could use the base services plus live with her parents. Sheila's Mom and Dad were real lifesavers; they welcomed Sheila back home even though she had three brothers plus a baby sister still at home.

CHAPTER 1

JUNE 1964

The Trip Over

June 5, 1964 Sheila and her parents drove me out to Wichita Mid Continental Airport where we said our goodbyes. I boarded a Continental Super Constellation Aircraft, flying stand by, headed for Albuquerque where I was to change planes to Las Vegas and then on to San Francisco. On the flight from Wichita, I met Jim another U.S. Air Force member; he was also heading to Travis AFB then on to Vietnam.

When we arrived in New Mexico we were informed that the aircraft to Las Vegas was full and we were both flying on standby so we would have to wait until the next flight. There was a brand new Boeing 707 four engine Jet sitting out on the ramp that we were supposed to be on. At the Albuquerque Airport they didn't have boarding ramps that you walk out in to board the aircraft like they do now. You had to pass through a fence gate where a stewardess would check your ticket then let you through the gate. Then you walked across the ramp and then up the stairs into the aircraft.

Boeing 707

    The stewardess that was checking everybody at the gate told us to wait until the last minute and she would check the plane to see if someone didn't show up, and if so she would get us on the aircraft. About that time here came a short, chubby guy with a well-dressed lady, "his secretary". They were on their way to Las Vegas, seeing that we were in uniform he stopped to talk to us asking where we were headed. We told him we were going to San Francisco then on to Vietnam, but we couldn't get on this flight because we were flying stand by and the plane was full. He then went over to the stewardess and talked to her for a minute and then came back to where we were waiting and told us to come with him. We went across the ramp then up the steps into this brand new Boeing 707 and instead of turning right to go to the back of the airplane, we turned left into a special first class section. There were beautiful couches and about 10 or 15 seats. It was really plush with coffee tables and lamps. The guy owned a large company in Omaha, Nebraska and he and his secretary were on their way to meetings in Las Vegas. They were flying 1st class, just to Las Vegas, and he worked out a deal with the head stewardess and the Captain to allow us to stay in 1st class all the way to San Francisco. After we were in the air the co-pilot came back and sat down with us and had a cup of coffee and asked us where we were going. He then took us into the cockpit and introduced us to the Captain and Flight Engineer. We talked to them for 10 or 15 minutes and then went back to our seats. They said they would let us know when we went over the Grand Canyon and we could go back up in the cockpit and check it out through the front of the aircraft instead of looking out a side window. AWESOME is all I could say! We then flew over Lake Mead before we landed in Las Vegas. We stayed on the airplane while they unloaded and loaded up for San Francisco. The head stewardess also brought an Army guy to ride up front with us; he also was headed for Vietnam. We ate steak and drank scotch and soda on the way to Frisco. I do not remember the guy from Omaha's name but he was quite a lifesaver for us. I have often wondered if it wasn't the billionaire Warren Buffett.

We landed in San Francisco and Jim and I caught a shuttle bus that ran from Travis AFB to the airport. I checked into the transient barracks, and then the next day, June 7th, I boarded a U.S.A.F. C-135 cargo plane converted to a troop transport. It is a 4-engine jet just like a Boeing 707 but for the military. The seats were mounted facing the back of the aircraft so you rode backwards. There were no windows except for two little portholes in the escape doors over the wings. I have never been in a submarine but now I can relate, there were 80 of us on the airplane and we would line up to take turns looking out the port holes.

You couldn't see anything but the wing and the Pacific Ocean, 40,000 feet below. We left Travis AFB Sunday morning at 9:00am headed for Hickam Field in Honolulu, Hawaii. It took 5 hours to fly 1700 miles and we arrived at 11:00am Honolulu time. When we came down from altitude to land at Hickam Field, a cloud formed in the aircraft and it rained, WEIRD. We arrived at 11am Honolulu time, a three-hour time difference. We got off the airplane and waited around for them to service the aircraft and to head for an 11 hour flight to Clark AFB in the Philippines.

Then they called all of us into a large room and told us that a bunch of cadets were on their way back to the states and they were having engine trouble with their airplane. They informed us that they were taking our airplane and we would have to stay in Hawaii for a couple of days, until our aircraft got back. You should have heard the cheers from 80 troops not looking forward to 11 more hours on that submarine. I met a guy named Chuck on the airplane and he and I checked into the same room in the transient barracks, we hung out that afternoon on the base and the

Airman's club that night. The next morning they told us our aircraft would not be back until the next day, so we changed clothes and caught a bus for Honolulu, about 5 miles from the base. We brought our bathing suits with us and got off at Waikiki Beach.

We walked up the beach for a mile or so, watching the people surf on Waikiki Beach and walking in front of all those plush, huge hotels. All the hotels are about 40 stories tall and built right on the beach overlooking the Pacific Ocean and Pearl Harbor. Chuck was from Las Angeles, California and was an experienced surfer. We had also hooked up with four other guys from the bunch and Chuck was going to teach us to surf. We rented surfboards for $1 apiece for all day long. I grew up on a lake in Michigan, and learned to water ski when I was 12 and was quite good at it but this was a first for me and the other guys, too. Chuck had to show us how to catch a wave. We paddled out into the ocean about a quarter of a mile; you should have seen the size of those waves! They scared the crap out of me and I wasn't sure if I wanted to ride one of those 7-foot waves to shore or not. Anyway, he showed us how to catch the wave, which is quite a trick. I missed about the first four waves, but I got on the fifth one and rode it almost all the way to shore, laying down, of course, not standing yet. Boy, was that ever fun, you ride right on the crest of the wave and it scares the heck out of you, because you can see the sand when you get close to shore, but if you fall you wouldn't hit the sand because there is a back suction just ahead of the wave and it will suck you right back into the water. Anyway, we paddled all the way back out there and it took me six waves to get one. A great big one, it must have been ten or twelve foot high and I rode this one all the way to the beach laying down, of course. I hadn't risen up enough nerve to stand up yet, or should I say try and stand up. So back out we went and this time I found me a little wave to try and stand up on. I caught the wave and was lying down and real slow I proceeded to stand up. I finally got up and went about 40ft and away I went, head over heels into that wave; it tossed me around like I was a feather. When it was done tossing me head over heels and I was half drowned, my surfboard was half way to the beach, so I had to swim after it. By the way, Chuck, the guy teaching us wasn't doing any better. He hadn't made it to shore standing up either. Back out we went, by this time I was getting pretty good at getting onto those waves. I found a smaller wave and this time I stood up and rode the wave all the way to the beach. After that I only fell off five or six times and we must have paddled out there twenty-five or thirty times. The guy that was trying to teach us only made it to shore five or six times, so I was doing pretty well. I was right out there with the best of them. Two native Hawaiians said I was doing real well, for the first time I have ever surfed, plus it was the first time I had ever been swimming in the ocean. They said I had good form for my first time. It sure was a lot of fun and to this day I have never surfed again.

We left the beach and started to walk into the main part of town. We found this place called the central marketing place, all it was, was a bunch of little shops built around a beautiful garden. It had a big Banyan tree right in the middle and the tree had a cocktail lounge built in the top of it, they called it the Tree House. We went up there and had a drink, scotch and 7-up, and you could see everything going on from up there. We came down out of the tree and walked around the market place where we saw where they were getting ready for a Luau. It was a private party and the guard at the entrance asked us if we were in the military. We told him we were on our way to Vietnam. He told us to wait and he went and talked to the person the Luau was for and came back and said we were invited to join the party. Of course we said, "Great". We had free food and booze the rest of the night. There was a stage where hula girls were dancing and very friendly wealthy people who let us join their party. We stayed about three hours, and then caught a bus back to Hickam Field. We got off at the airman's club and had a few beers. By this time I was beat, because the night before when we got into San Francisco, it was 1:00 in the morning before I got into bed and I got up at 5:00am. I did get some sleep on the airplane to Hawaii the night before. It was a long day because I'd been chasing the sun all the way. All that paddling I did with the surf board all day wore me out, too. I guess it was midnight when I got into bed and I got up at 6:00am to catch the flight to Clark A.F.B. in Manila at 8:00am.

Now, here we are all 80 of us back on that flying submarine on our way to Clark AFB in the Philippines. They say it will take us 11 hours to fly from Hickam Field in Honolulu to Clark AFB. Non-stop it is 6000 miles. The aircraft commander announced that we could come up front and watch them fly the airplane two at a time. It did give us something to do, plus we had some card games going that I could get in on. I spent about 30 minutes with the flight crew up front. We were flying at 39,000 feet with a ground speed of 605 miles per hour. They just sat there drinking coffee and talking, the airplane was flying itself on autopilot. They were really happy to talk with us because they were just as bored as we were. Trying to keep up with time was a real problem. Flying from Honolulu to Manila we lost six hours, plus somewhere between Hawaii and the Philippines is the International Date Line. In Hawaii it was Wednesday, but in Manila is was Thursday Oh well, I didn't quite understand it but I took their word for it. Ha

We arrived at Clark AFB and checked into the transient barracks and went to bed and slept for ten hours. The next morning I attended an orientation class and had more shots. UGH! After lunch those of us that were going to Vietnam had to re-qualify on the firing range. I had qualified in boot camp when I joined the U.S. Air Force. We used a World War II, M-1 automatic rifle. We sure were surprised when they brought out the brand new AR-15 automatic weapon, later to become the M-16. Wow, what a weapon, we were amazed when they demonstrated what it would do.

They stacked up some cement blocks two deep and about 5 feet tall. One of the instructors had a backpack holding the ammunition and a belt of ammunition running into where the 30 round ammunition magazine would normally go. His backpack held 200 rounds and he opened up on that stack of bricks and in two minutes that concrete was reduced to rubble. It was a great firing weapon and I qualified very well with it. You could launch grenades from it and the first one they tried was a dud and only went twenty yards. It's a good thing we had a sand bag revetment foxhole to jump into. It didn't explode, thank God, but they had to call the bomb disposal guys to come get it.

The next day at Clark AFB all I had to do was find a ride to Saigon, which, I did, but it didn't leave until 4:00pm. I had to hang around base operations till then and it was only 10:00am. I knew I was going to Saigon to work on a secret project with B-57 Reconnaissance aircraft as a mechanic. There must have been 50 B-57 Fighter Bombers on the ramp at Clark AFB. I had a lot of time to kill, so I wandered out on the flight line to see what I could learn about the B-57 aircraft. I hooked up with a couple of mechanics assigned to them. When I told them where I was headed and what I would be doing, they knew about the two airplanes in Saigon because they would work on them when they came to Clark AFB for their 100-hour inspection, then send them back to Saigon.

USAF B-57

I stayed with them all day; they took me to lunch with them and filled me in on what they were doing at Clark AFB. There were 50 B-57 aircraft, 2 squadrons of 25 all maintaining combat ready status. The defense department moved the wing from Tokyo to Manila about six weeks ago and they returned all their dependents to the U.S. They are training at Clark AFB on the bombing range but have not been given a specific target. They believe they are training in the Philippines to bomb targets in Communist North Vietnam. I would later meet up with some of their airplanes in Saigon; I will explain what happened later. On the Clark AFB flight line were a bunch of F-100 Jet fighters also, F-102 Interceptors as well as the B-57's. All of them are maintaining combat ready status.

At 4:00pm I boarded a C-54 Cargo plane that was going to Saigon, then on to Bangkok. There were no seats only a few jump seats along the sides of the airplane. The plane was full of cargo and I was the only passenger besides the crew; the Pilot, Co-pilot, Engineer, the aircraft Crew Chief and a Loadmaster.

This was Saturday, June 13, 1964. When I was not in the cockpit with the crew I took a nap on a pile of tents in the back. The C-54 Cargo plane is a 4 engine, piston driven plane. It was just turning dark when we landed at Tan Son Nhut Airfield, Saigon, South Vietnam. We taxied up in front of base operations where they would unload part of the cargo. I got off the aircraft and went into the operations building and the first thing I see is a rat the size of a small dog run across the room. The guy at the desk said not to worry they weren't all that big, this one was their pet so he is well fed! They loaded me up in a Jeep and took me to the 5 Star hotels they had there at the base, a huge "Tent City".

I checked in at the officer of the day tent and was assigned a tent with 3 other guys. We all lived together, Army, Navy, Marine and Air Force. I was really glad to have two Army roommates as they had guns. Another Air Force guy that worked in the Air Force Squadron Orderly Room as a clerk was also one of my roommates. His name was Joe (I don't remember his last name). We were good friends until he left; I think it was March of 1965 when he went home.

The tents were set up on wooden platforms and there were wooden walkways between the tents. It was like streets and had a latrine with showers on each block. There were probably 300 tents, big, four man tents, and it was a regular city. (I was lucky and moved into one of the brand new barracks a few weeks later). I didn't have to report to work on the flight line until Monday morning and it was Saturday night when I arrived so I had some time to kill.

Our new barracks

That night I could hear the 105 Howitzers in the distance and it was the same almost every night I was in Vietnam. I don't think I got any sleep that night listening to those explosions all night.

Tan Son Nhut Airbase

Sunday, June 14, 1964 I spent the whole day just looking around Tan Son Nhut Airfield. This is a new base that they are just getting built.

Our new chow hall

We have a new Chow Hall, Movie Theater and an Airman's club that is real nice and they are building new buildings all over the base. Most of the enlisted men live in tents and most of the officers live downtown Saigon in real nice hotels. This worked out very well for some of us because our pilots were also our friends and they would let us sleep on their couch or the floor when we were in town if we couldn't make it back to base before curfew.

The Base was quite safe also. There are 5,000 Vietnam Government troops guarding the base and a 24-hour helicopter patrol going around the base perimeter. There were at least a hundred Hu-1(Huey) helicopters, about 60 C-123 twin engine cargo aircraft that had multiple uses. There were 12 RF-101 Reconnaissance jets and 2 RB-57 Reconnaissance bombers parked in a special jet parking area. Also a bunch of old World War II A1H and A1E fighter bombers that were assigned to the South Vietnamese Air Force. I would be working on the 2 RB-57's. Plus there were about every other type of aircraft that was ever made coming and going. There was only one runway, although there was a parallel runway under construction. This made Tan Son Nhut Airfield, Saigon the busiest airport in the world!

I thought it was miserable hot in Georgia in the summer time but it was worse in Vietnam. It is the rainy season from May through October and the daytime temperature can reach 110 degrees in the shade and it is extremely humid. At night it does get nice and cool so it isn't so bad, although you have to sleep with mosquito nets over your bunk. Some of those mosquitoes were so big, one of them landed on the ramp and we put 50 gallons of fuel in it before we figured out what it was.

Monday morning, June 15, 1964, I caught a ride over to the flight line and reported to work. The jet parking ramp is located at the far end of the parking ramp at the east end of the runway next to the Air Vietnam civilian hangers. There was an old stone and brick house that our pilots used as an Operations Office. There was also a 10 ft. by 40 ft. air conditioned house trailer that was our Maintenance Office. There were also several tents that the camera people and armament people used. There was 1 tent where the film readers looked at the pictures we took with our aircraft.

I reported to our detachment commander, Major Musgrove, who is also the Chief Pilot. I was also introduced to the other flight crews. We have 3 crews, Major Musgrove and Captain Cobb, his navigator, Major McGinnis and Captain Young, his navigator and Major Stanfield and Lt. Platt, his navigator. The first thing I noticed was the difference between being at a base in the States and a base in a war zone. Major Musgrove informed me that we were quite informal and if we run into each other when we were in Saigon, we were to use first or last names only. (Lt. Platt and I became good friends while we were in Vietnam and hung out at the airman's club and Saigon quite often, he was only 2 years older than me). They didn't want the locals to know they were officers. Major Musgrove informed me of how important our mission was and said that we had top priority on the base, in other words we got anything we asked for. The two RB-57E aircraft I would be working on were the most important aircraft in all of Vietnam and remained that way throughout the Vietnam War. They are serial numbers 55-4243 and 55-4245.

Then I met Master Sergeant Cogdill, the maintenance boss. We didn't get along very well at first. We had 1 Master Sergeant, 1 Tech Sergeant, 3 Staff Sergeants and one Airman Second Class, ME! I don't know what they did before I arrived; I got all the crap details. I did ALL the work and the rest of the guys sat around in the air-conditioned maintenance office and looked over my shoulder. The maintenance office had two bedrooms that Master Sergeant Cogdill and Tech Sergeant Gibson lived in because it was air-conditioned. It was great during the day when the airplanes were flying, but when they landed, the guys would yell, Karmes! So I would go out and park it, refuel it and inspect it while they sat around in the air-conditioned trailer. I was also the water boy because we had no water hooked up in the trailer. When the water jug was empty they would yell, Karmes! And I would go fill it; this happened at least five times a day. I had to get in the truck and drive all the way up to base operations to fill it and then back.

Looking across the ramp is the pilot's operation building and our maintenance trailer

The boss was Master Sergeant Cogdill and he rode me like a rented donkey. Later, he and I became good friends; he was the best boss I have ever worked for to this very day. Tech Sergeant Gibson, Staff Sergeant Gilmore, Staff Sergeant Ware and Staff Sergeant Davis were also part of the crew. Later, after about five weeks, Major Musgrove called me into his office along with Sgt Cogdill and explained to me why they had been having me do most of the work. The rest of the guys were training me. The guys were all leaving the 1st of August and there would be only Sgt.Cogdill, Sgt Ware and Me. They didn't know when or if we would be getting help and when we did get help I would have to help train them. They would probably be higher in rank than me, but they would be working for me. After that meeting things changed drastically, I was accepted as the Crew Chief on Aircraft 55-4245. I no longer had to do ALL of the work, actually I didn't do ALL the work before, but it seemed like it. We were a very close knitted bunch, the pilots, the Aircraft Maintenance bunch and the Camera and Armament guys.

245 on the taxiway (My picture)

243 on the parking ramp Air Vietnam hangers are in the background

The Awesome B-57 Aircraft

The Martin B-57 Canberra is a United States built, twin jet engine light bomber and reconnaissance aircraft. It entered service with the United States Air Force in 1953. The B-57 was initially a version of the English Electric Canberra, built in the USA under license by the Glen L Martin Company. The Martin B-57 is a significantly modified designed, and they produced several variants. Ours were B-57E models that were modified to all weather reconnaissance aircraft designated RB-57E models and used in the Secret "Patricia Lynn" project in Vietnam.

Though intended as a light bomber the B-57 had never been deployed by the Air Force to a combat zone. The first two B-57s to be deployed to South Vietnam were not operated in an offensive role, although we changed that later. I will tell you about our one and only weapon later. Our two RB-57Es were modified for special reconnaissance missions and assigned to the 405th fighter wing at Clark AFB in the Philippines, then to Detachment 1 of the 33 tactical group Tan Son Nhut Airfield at Saigon South Vietnam in May of 1963, becoming the first jet aircraft assigned to Vietnam.

The modifications of the B-57E were performed by the General Dynamics Company in Fort Worth Texas, rather than the Martin Company and were called the "Patricia Lynn" project, after the design engineer's wife's name. The modifications included altering the aircraft nose to house a 36-inch KA-1 forward oblique camera and a KA-56 panoramic camera. Mounted within the modified bomb bay area were a KA-1 camera mounted in the vertical position, a K-477 vertical "Day-Night" camera, and a KA-1 camera mounted as a port facing oblique.

The need for additional reconnaissance assets especially those capable of operating at night resulted in these two aircraft being equipped with Infrared coverage using the secret "Reconofax 1V" Infrared cameras also located in the modified bomb bay. I don't know what all those numbers mean but I do know that all that equipment was state of the art at that time. The Patricia Lynn Aircraft was used throughout the war as a test platform for the latest camera equipment.

The lengthened nose gave the aircraft a distinctive appearance compared to the other models of B-57's. Also there are 80 photo flash cartridges built into a special rack under the belly of the aircraft. They have a timer in them, so two seconds after they leave the aircraft they go off and they fire them from the aircraft two seconds apart. It was quite a sight to see; when in the distance we could see when the aircraft took pictures at night. The aircraft was about five miles north of the base and running with no lights on. It looked like a big flash camera in the sky when they went across the target, so all you could see is a big flash one right after another. They lit up the whole sky for a fraction of a second, the pictures taken that way look like they were taken in the day.

The first two aircraft, serial numbers 55-4243 and 55-4245 were not painted, later they were painted black for better night operations. In January of 1965 we received two more modified RB-57E's serial numbers 55-4237 and 55-4249, they also were not painted black. A fifth aircraft was received in November of 1965 serial number 55-4264. These five aircraft formed, detachment 1 of the 460th tactical reconnaissance wing (earlier the 6250th tactical group), earlier still the 33rd tactical group which I was assigned to. I was the crew chief on aircraft 55-4245 and later in January aircraft 55-4249 although we all worked on all the aircraft.

On a typical mission our aircraft would fly over the Mekong delta monitoring river traffic. Also the panhandle, the DMZ, and other classified areas like Laos, Cambodia, and North Vietnam. We would locate enemy forces and material being moved southward at night into South Vietnam using our infrared cameras. Also after an air strike the "Patricia Lynn" aircraft would complete a bomb damage assessment run over the previous attacked target area. Eighty percent of all the usable air intelligence collected in the Vietnam War came from the five "Patricia Lynn" aircraft assigned to the Detachment -1 wing at Tan Son Nhut airfield. Most of our targets were along the Ho Chi Minh trail and the canals down in the Mekong river delta, later also all of North Vietnam plus some places they should not be in.

Like I said the Ho Chi Minh Trail was where our two aircraft spent a lot of their time monitoring the movement of troops and equipment. We would fly over the trails at night and use the in-fra red camera to locate the enemy camps. Then when our aircraft landed and the film was looked at they would send out the A-1H propeller driven fighter bombers to bomb strafe and drop napalm on the camps and the approaches to the trails in Laos.

The Hoe Chi Minh Trail starts in North Vietnam and winds down through Laos by a network of foot paths. Then it fans out into South Vietnam along the Laos border into a spider web of trails that are very difficult to find. But our aircraft could find them, we could pick up the heat from their camp fires and we would know which way they were traveling and approximately how many.

The trails were first used against the French during the Indochina war in Southeast Asia from 1950 to 1954. Then in 1962 the communists won the war for Laos when they managed to win control of the areas embracing the Ho Chi Minh trail. Later in 1963 US reconnaissance aircraft (our Patricia Lynn RB- 57E aircraft) on night patrol noticed numerous campfires using their infrared cameras along the trail. Then they monitored them each night and the fires moved south. In this last year bombing of the access roads to the Ho Chi Minh trail has been stepped up. Nobody believes it's going to stop the communist traffic so all they can do is keep harassing them. Our Pilots say because of the nature of the network of paths and trails they change constantly from year to year or season to season which makes the job difficult to keep monitoring the trails. The only way to stop the traffic would be to bring in many troops but that would not work either. Our brave Pilots spent many hours monitoring the Ho Chi Minh trail while I was there.

For eight years starting in 1963 our camera packed RB-57E platform sported the latest in electronic surveillance equipment. Just about every time we would send one of our aircraft over to Clark AFB for its 100 hour inspection it would come back with something new on it. In 1970 the Military Assistance Command Vietnam (MACV) credited Detachment-1 at Tan Son Nhut air base with providing more than 94% of the battlefield intelligence; this included the other models of recon aircraft that were later assigned.

The RB-57E was a great aircraft to maintain, we would fly for hours before we had any problems, a bad generator or a defective shotgun starter was the biggest problem we had. Occasionally we would change an engine, tire or brakes, but mostly minor problems except for the battle damage that every one of them received. I will tell you about the damage we received the year I was there as it happened. Every 100 hours of flying time we would send the aircraft to Clark AFB in the Philippines where they would inspect every inch of the aircraft. They would install new engines, any new state of the art camera equipment and anything else the aircraft needed, then send it back to us. All we had to do was refuel it, take care of the pre-flight, post-flight inspections and repair any minor problems and any rare major problems that developed.

The crews consisted of the pilot (the only one with the flight controls) and behind him in the rear seat the navigator-camera operator. Later in the war a TV screen was installed in the rear where the camera operator could see in real time what the Infrared camera was recording. This was a great improvement because he could call an air strike immediately, rather than after the aircraft landed and the film was inspected. When I was there we did not have that improvement until later just before I left. When the aircraft would land the camera people would unload the film and rush it to the area where they would develop it and read it. One of the guys that work on the Infra-red explained it to me this way. I don't quite understand it yet but he said it doesn't actually take a picture; it just picks up the light radiation from the ground as the aircraft flies over. He showed me some film my aircraft took and it showed clearly the jungle and rivers. Then in some parts there are little specks of light, he said they were Viet Cong camp fires or hot truck engines. That is how they find them in the jungle because the Infra-Red picks up the radiation right through the jungle.

After our aircraft would land and the film was looked at, then we would watch the old WW-II A-1H and A-1E Fighter Bombers loaded with bombs come screaming down the taxiway and take off. During the rainy season they were having problems with the bombs not exploding until they were deep in the ground. To fix it they would weld a piece of pipe or an old machine gun barrel to the nose fuse of the bomb; they really looked weird coming down the taxiway with all that junk sticking out in front of the wings.

A1H Sky Rader

The B-57 aircraft length is 65ft from nose to tail the wingspan is 64ft. The wing area is 960sq ft, kind of like a ballroom dance floor, it is huge. The engines are two Wright J65-W-5 turbojet engines each one providing 7,220 lbs of thrust. The maximum speed is 595 mph, and the combat radius is 950 miles.

The engines use what is called a pyrotechnic cartridge starter (we call it a shotgun starter). The cartridge is vacuum packed in what looks like a 3-pound coffee can. The starter assembly is located in the center of the engine air intake in front of the engine. When the cartridge is fired it produces a copious amount of black smoke, from a distance you would swear the aircraft is blowing up. When the engines start and sits at idle you need good ear protection because they make a woo woo sound that you can feel through your whole body.

B-57 Engine start

The aircraft holds 2,300 gallons of jet fuel, including the wing tip tanks. Refueling takes over one hour. The infrared camera was quite remarkable, at one point we tested the system by Major Musgrove flying over the flight line and taking a picture of itself sitting on the ramp. Just the difference in temperature of where it was parked would show a perfect outline of the airplane sitting on the parking ramp. On another occasion 5 of us stood in a circle on the ramp at night smoking a cigarette and one of the base commanders that lived just off base in a Villa built a small fire in his back yard. The system worked perfectly showing each heat source. The Viet Cong were not safe anywhere our airplanes flew especially at night.

Two RB57Es were lost in combat operations. The first (S/N 55-4243) (3 months after I left Vietnam in August of 1965) it was lost as a result of a fuselage fire caused by small arms while on a low level reconnaissance mission. The crew ejected safely when near Tan Son Nhut air base. The second aircraft (S/N 55-4264) was lost on Oct. 15, 1968 after an engine fire caused by ground fire forced the crew to eject. Our pilots were, in my opinion, some of the bravest solders in all of Vietnam. They would fly our aircraft at tree top level at slow speeds taking small arms fire on almost every mission. One more RB57E was converted as a replacement for the combat losses. The "Patricia Lynn" aircraft continued flying combat missions until they were withdrawn in mid-1971.

Also 12 RF101 (Voo Doo) reconnaissance jets had just arrived from Kadena Air Force Base Okinawa Japan. They are parked on the jet parking ramp along with our airplanes. They are here on 90-day temporary duty with their pilots and the crews to maintain them. They use the same resources we use except they do not have an air-conditioned maintenance office, they had to use a tent. We did let them visit us in our air conditioned trailer any time they needed to cool off. The RF-101 is also quite an aircraft although it doesn't have infrared cameras like our aircraft. They have a short black nose that has a camera in it plus one on each side of the nose and two under the belly straight under the cockpit. It has two J-57 engines with after burners and will go like a streak twice the speed of sound plus.

RF-101 (Voo Doo) on the ramp in 1964

Here is some information about the Indochina peninsula in 1964 that the air Force gave us when we arrived in South Vietnam.

The Indochina Peninsula is 450 miles wide and over 500 miles in length; it juts out from continental Asia southeastward into the South China Sea. Burma and Thailand occupy the western part of the peninsula; the southern and eastern parts constitute the region that until 1954 was known as "French Indochina". This region now consisted of four politically separate and independent states. CAMBODIA with its capital at Pnompenh is a kingdom of 67,571 square miles and a population of about 5 million. LAOS, with its administrative capital at Vientiane and the royal capital at Luang Prabang, is a kingdom of 91,503 square miles and a population of 2 million. NORTH VIETNAM with its capital at Hanoi is a republic of 64,000 square miles and a population of 13 million. SOUTH VIETNAM with its capital at Saigon is a republic of 66,500 square miles and a population of 12 million. South Vietnam occupies the southern portion of the rugged Annamese Cordillera Mountains, which exceeds 7,300 feet near the city of Dalat, and the vast lowlands of the Mekong delta, which are crisscrossed by a maze of natural and manmade waterways. Before it enters South Vietnam, the Mekong River has already divided into two great distributaries, the Mekong proper and the Bassac, which flow in roughly parallel courses to the sea.

The climate is tropical monsoon with copious rainfall (80 inches in Saigon), which falls principally from May through October. Mean monthly temperatures at Saigon range from 79 degrees in December and January to 85 degrees in April. Natural vegetation is mostly evergreen rain and swamp forest, although much of the delta has been cleared for rice cultivation. Elephant, tigers, deer, bear, water buffalo, and game birds are common in the highlands. The soils of the Mekong delta are rich and the area has long been one of the great rice-exporting regions of Southeast Asia. Rice, corn and sweet potatoes are the chief subsistence crops. After World War II, the French reconstituted the territory as the three associated states of Vietnam, Cambodia, and Laos but they were unable to re-establish their hold over Northern Vietnam. Since the Geneva Agreement of 1954, South Vietnam has been fully independent. By the provisions of the constitution of October 1956, South Vietnam is a democratic republic, headed by a president. There is an elected legislative assembly.

Saigon-Cholon are twin cities with 1.8 million people separated by a wide avenue. Saigon is the capital and chief port for South Vietnam as well as the main port for Cambodia and Laos; Cholon is the commercial city. Saigon is famous for the beauty of its broad tree-lined avenues and the French architecture of its buildings. The exchange rate of dollars to South Vietnam Peastra is approximately 73 Pea to one dollar. U.S. Personnel stationed in Saigon were limited to $100.00 per month in U.S. currency at the time I was there. Although in downtown Saigon you could exchange your dollars illegally for up to 130 Pea to one dollar. Later after I left, U.S. Personnel were paid in Script because of this.

Downtown Saigon 1964

My first trip to Saigon

My first weeks on the base I spent getting things set up; I moved into the barracks, had more shots UGH and located everything on the base that I needed. Then I decided to check out Saigon, I got on an Air Force bus that made scheduled trips to downtown Saigon and Cholon. I rode the bus all the way downtown and back, I never got off I just went on sort of a tour. It took us about an hour and a half to go downtown, make all the stops and come back to Tan Son Nhut. Town starts right at the edge of the base. There are a lot of beautiful old and new buildings and you can see the French influence and of course they have their share of slums also. You would never know these people are in the middle of a war. They smile at you and say hi, that's about the only English most of them know although some of them can speak English quite well. They all go out of their way to help you and everybody on the base goes out of their way to help them. They are real friendly to Americans.

I sure wouldn't like to ride a bike or drive a car down there; they all drive like they are crazy. It's a wonder our bus didn't run someone down; they don't even look where they are going they just go. The biggest vehicle has the right of way, even if it is pulling out of an ally onto a major street. Everyone and their brother have a bike or a motorbike and they ride right down the middle of the street and they won't move no matter what's coming.

Here is a piece on Saigon traffic that one of the guys in the barracks had put up on the bulletin board. I copied it and sent it home to Sheila in a letter. It sums it all up and is pretty funny.

A big city traffic cop, after saving for years and with the help of the friendly bookie on his beat, goes on a world tour, and returns. He is sitting around the station house, gassing with the boys, regaling them with tales of his travels.

"Saigon, aah, Saigon," he reminisces. "That was the wildest." A cop in that town couldn't get by with a hundred pads of tickets a day; he tells them "Ya'd need a mule to drag enough along." "Listen, they got these little bicycles with three wheels anna guy up top peddling. Supposed to hold one passenger on a seat in front. I seen five passengers, ten chickens, anna pig in one. With one little guy peddlin', mind ya. No horn, no lights, and darn little brakes. Wants t' turn he flops his arm in the breeze an' turns. Just like that. Forty thousan' cars comin' down the street, and he does a "U" turn because one of his passengers drops a penny, see?

"Know what? They got these carts with cows pullin' em, see? Ya, cows, right in the middle of it all. And more carts with little ponies draggin' em. It's like Walt Disney invented a whole bunch of new rides. Honest.

"Taxis? Have they got taxis I'll tellya they got 'em. Bout a million I'd say. Little French bugs painted blue and white, but not painted quite as slick as the president's jet. Looks t' me like the only thing that has to work on 'em is the meter and the horn. Maybe the motor, sometimes, too. "The taxis, an' alla the other traffic go around these circles inna middle of the streets, see, bout a hundred miles an hour. Looks like a midget Inna-apolis race. Ever'body just tooting their horns like crazy and waving their arms.

Sure they got more. They got all these bikes. Looks like every kind of bike ever made in the world is onna streets. They got all these bikes. Looks like every kind from the ones you have t' pump plus them big Harleys, some of em even have a little motor on the front wheel. Always somebody on the back…. Usually a young chick. They got these long skirts see, spilt alla way up, with silk slacks under. Anna skirts blow inna breeze, which blinds the guy on the bike behind 'em.

"Listen you non-travelled boobs. Didya ever see six people onna a motor scooter without a sidecar? Yeah, well they do it all the time. One driving, two sittin', lap on lap on the back, and three standing' between the handlebars on the little floor there in the front of the driver. The biggest vehicle has the right of way, so if yer driven one of those big six by trucks, you can pull out of an ally, an' you don't even have to look. Just pull out and go.

"The pedestrians are something' else, too. When they wanna cross a street, they cross the thing, an' it don't matter none what else happens t' be in the street. Like if it was a tank coming down the road full blower, the tank'd have t' stop, else run 'em over. One thing about them jays, however, they always signal the driver to stop and get out of the way. And when one goes, then a million follow and all the traffic has to stop.

If you are reading this and spent some time In Saigon in the sixties you will relate, and I would say it was even worse.

French Fiat taxies Downtown Saigon

There are guards all over the place and thick screens on all the bars and a guard out in front of most of them. We went by where a ship had been sunk by the Viet Cong in the river and the Hollywood bar where they tried to throw a bomb in; but it hit the screen and bounced out into the street and exploded. By the way the bus driver is giving me all this information, it seems that almost everybody new on the base take their first trip to Saigon with him and he likes to think he is a tour guide. He said that last week an Air Force Air Police sergeant had a flat tire downtown and he had his truck jacked up and the tire off when a guy came by on a bike and threw a bomb in the back. He jumped in the ditch and shot the guy just as the bomb exploded and blew up his truck. I later came to find out that Saigon and Cholon are quite safe if you are careful. I spent many hours exploring Saigon the year I was in South Vietnam, I will write about some of them later.

Saigon Police (White Mice)

Trip to Vung Tau

When I got back from Saigon I ran into my buddy Joe over at the airman's club, the guy I lived with in the tent city that works in the squadron orderly room. He asked me if I wanted to go to the beach down at Vung Tau on the South China Sea on Sunday. There is an aircraft that will leave at 9 am and can take 30 people. It seems he is in charge of the sign up list and he put both of our names at the top of the list. I am off on Sunday so I agreed. He said the C-123 aircraft named Patches would be parked in front of base operations and to be there at eight thirty Sunday morning. The Australians have a base down there and there is a real nice beach there, they call it the French Riviera of Vietnam. I arrived at the airplane on Sunday and immediately knew why they call it Patches. The airplane is what they call a Ranch Hand over here; it is what they use to spray the jungle with Agent Orange poison to kill the foliage along the Cambodia and Laos border so the patrol aircraft can see the enemy when they cross. They fly low over the jungle and are hit with small arms fire on almost every mission. When they patch the holes they paint them red and this airplane was covered with hundreds of red patches. The Ranch Hand aircraft was shot at and hit more frequently than any other Air Force aircraft in the Vietnam War. The crew compartment up front is protected with steel reinforcement to protect them. We have four of these aircraft here in Vietnam, later more were added. One of the guys in the barracks is a crew chief on one of these aircraft. He says that when they fly a mission they will have with them an Army medical evacuation helicopter, two Air Force rescue choppers and from 6 to 8 South Vietnamese Air Force A-1 H Sky Raiders. They fly 150 feet above the jungle when they spray and when they get down that low the crew chief climbs up into the cockpit where the reinforcement is with the pilots. He says they take along plenty of protection just in case they are shot down which has not happened as to this date. Although they have lost an engine on several occasions but only one and they still have one engine to get back to the base.

During research on this book I found out that the Ranch Hand Patches a VC-123K (serial number 56-4362) is on display at the Air Force Museum in Ohio. Many metal skin patches cover the damage of its over 1000 battle hits.

When I arrived at the plane, the cargo ramp was lowered in the back and inside is a large tank that holds the Agent Orange, a pump and lines that run out to spray bars under the wings. There are 30 jump seats that run along the sides of the airplane facing the tank. We all loaded up and got a seat and about ten minutes later here come two guys wearing tee shirts, bathing suites, and flip flops on their feet. They walked up the ramp and said are you guys ready to go, we all hollered yes and they climbed up into the cockpit. I guess they were the pilots because they cranked up the engines and off we went. The flight took us 20 minutes to fly down there and when we got there the pilots wanted to see how crowded the beach was. So we dove down and found out. We were so low I could have reached out and shook hands with the people on the beach. We were so low water from the propeller wash was coming in the back because we flew down there with the back ramp down. After we buzzed the beach we landed at the base about 2 miles away from the beach. The pilots neglected to tell us that we are landing on a PSP runway (perforated steel planks) they hook together kind of like legoes. We thought the airplane was going to vibrate apart when we hit that runway; the perforated holes in the planks are about 6 or 8 inches around to allow for water drainage, but we made it OK. Then the Australians' loaded us onto a truck and took us to the Vung Tau beach.

The city of Vung Tau is a remarkable place that has beautiful buildings and a magnificent beach with white sand as far as you can see and then some. That's why they call it the French Riviera of South Vietnam. Situated on a tiny strip of land shaped like a thumb extending into the South China Sea near the southern end of the country. It has long been a place of escape and rest and relaxation. The resort beach had been a favorite getaway for the French colonials and the wealthy of Saigon since the late 19th century. During the Vietnam War, Vung Tau was a city of war and peace, serving as an important active port and as a favorite R&R spot for fighting men. But for most Americans Vung Tau is the most popular in country R&R destination in Vietnam. Not only was Vung Tau used by Americans, Australians, South Vietnamese and their allies as an R&R destination but even the Viet Cong would go to the city for some R&R of their own. I am sure we were swimming with them every time we were there.

The beach was awesome and there were two large hills or some called them mountains just off shore that protected the beach. The South China Sea is so salty you could lie out on your back in the water and take a nap and not sink. The darn sun didn't shine but about 30 minutes and we were there all day, but the radiation come through the clouds and boy did I get good sunburn.

We had lunch and drank Ba Muoi Ba beer in excess at one of the many bars on the beach. A note about that Ba Muoi Ba beer pronounced Bomb nee Ba, or sometime called beer 33, I think it is 33% alcohol and was made the day before, and it takes at least a month to get used to it to stop having the runs. Ha At 4 pm we loaded back up in patches and just as we were ready to take off a big storm blew up, so we waited for it to pass. It didn't let up so we took off anyway and buzzed the beach again before we headed back to Saigon.

CHAPTER 2

JULY 1964

First Firefight

I had been in Vietnam for a month now and I was sure it looked as if I had quite an adventure. It definitely had been an adventure, but that was about to change. There had been a firefight just off the west end of the runway. We were working that night and we could hear the gunfire real well even though we are at the east end of the runway. They shut down the runway and then several-armed Heuy helicopters appeared, firing rockets, 20 mm cannons and 50cal machine guns.

The C-123 aircraft were dropping flares and lighting up the whole world, you could see the 50cal machine guns red tracer bullets off in the distance. They looked like a wavering red line coming from the Heuy then to the ground. Some of these Heuy helicopters are well armed; they carry 2 rocket pods and 20mm cannons mounted on each side of the helicopter plus 2 manned 50cal machine guns sticking out of each door. They can do some real damage and the Viet Cong are really afraid of them. The fight lasted about 2 hours and 41 Viet Cong were killed, 29 South Vietnamese were killed and 2 US Army Special Forces advisors were killed. The next morning there were still some Viet Cong sitting right at the end of the west end of the runway shooting at the airplanes taking off, but the US Army took care of them in a hurry. After that the Army had to fly armed Heuy helicopters along side of the big jets like Pan American Boeing 707s and Northwest DC-8s because they couldn't get high enough on takeoff to be safe from ground fire.

Then to top it all off the next day we were on our way to the chow hall for lunch and they were unloading the bodies from that firefight and there were two body bags draped with American flags. We were in our Metro maintenance truck (looks like a bread truck) Sgt Cogdill, Sgt Ware and me. Sgt Ware was driving and Sgt Cogdill said stop the truck and get out. We got out and stood next to the truck as they loaded the two Americans in an ambulance. I looked over at Sgt Cogdill and tears were running down his cheeks. He looked at us and said that he considers every American soldier here in Viet Nam as one of his boys. After seeing those two flag draped body bags I knew this war was serious. We got back in the truck, turned around and went back to work, nobody was hungry after that. Later that day Sgt Ware and I talked about what had happened with Sgt Cogdill and from that day forward our attitude toward him changed. He was probably the greatest boss I ever worked for and he didn't change at all, but Sgt Ware and I did and that was the difference.

Sky Rader Crash

July 5, 1964

We were returning back to the flight line from the chow hall after lunch when we noticed the fire trucks were heading out to the runway. A South Vietnamese A-1 H Sky Rader fighter bomber was coming in on emergency so we stopped to watch.

We stopped the truck and watched him come across the field and over the tower so they could inform him of what battle damage he had. The right wing was severely damaged and we could see fuel leaking out of the wing. Also the right landing gear was only halfway down and the engine was smoking. Just as he passed over us the leaking fuel caught fire causing the whole right wing to be in flames. Sgt. Ware looked over at Sgt. Gogdill and said we better pray for that pilot as he has a big problem.

This guy was in real trouble and he knew there was no way he was going to land that aircraft. When he caught fire he climbed almost straight up to gain altitude. We watched him turn to the right toward an open area across the runway. He already had the canopy open and when he got high enough, we watched him climb out and jump. He made it out okay and his parachute opened with no problem. When he bailed out the aircraft nosed over and went straight down. By this time the whole aircraft was on fire and we watched this huge fireball go straight into the ground in an open area approximately half a mile away. There was a huge explosion and the aircraft was completely destroyed. Then we watched the pilot, (by the way, he was an American Pilot flying a South Vietnamese A-1 H Sky Rader), he slowly came down and the wind pushed him back over the runway, toward where we were watching. Then he landed in a grassy area between the runway and the taxiway. He didn't even fall down, he just stood there and released his parachute and walked over to where one of the fire trucks was parked. The firemen gathered up his parachute and an ambulance showed up but he was not injured at all. They were only about 30 yards from us, so we walked over to them and Sgt. Cogdill asked him if he was okay. I was amazed that he was so calm. He said he was on his strafing run about 20 miles south of Saigon and he flew into a hail of 50 caliber bullets. He said he didn't know if he would make it to Tan Son Nhut airfield, which was the closest or not. He was flying out of Bien Hoa (Ben Wa) airfield and he knew he couldn't make it back there, besides he did not want to bail out over Viet Cong territory if his engine failed. He expected his engine to quit at any minute but it kept running and he made it to Tan Son Nhut airfield okay. He said several bullets came right up through the cockpit floor but missed him.

Then they loaded him in the ambulance and took him over to the medical center on base. The fire department put out the fire on the crashed aircraft and the airfield was back in business. That was quite an interesting lunch hour and the first of the many crashes I would witness in the year I was in Viet Nam.

July 9, 10 and 11 we worked 14-hour days in two shifts, the reason was the weather up north (North Vietnam, Laos and along the border of Red China) was bad and we have some high priority targets we need to get. As soon as the pilots get briefed on what the weather is like up there they take off. We have been flying both aircraft 5 times a day and even the pilots have been coming out to help us get them ready. I wish I could have gotten a picture of Lt. Platt straddling a tip tank pumping fuel like one of the guys. We are beat, the pilots are beat and none of us are very happy with the weather but they say we have a good chance tonight because around 10:00 pm it's going to clear up and maybe they can get in there and get our pictures. That night we finally got the target and we sure were glad. Also the RF-101s were after that same target that we were and one of them got hit with a 30cal round in the gas tank. We sure were glad it was one of them and not one of ours because they have self-sealing gas tanks and we don't. Although it was one of the drop tanks that was empty so they replaced it, filled the aircraft with fuel and sent it back to North Vietnam.

Jet Parking Area 1964

The RF-101 Voo Doo is the fastest aircraft we have over here and it can get over North Vietnam and back in a hurry. A few days later that same aircraft was hit again in one of his drop tanks again, only this time it caught fire. The pilot ejected both tanks but only the one that was on fire separated from the aircraft that was a good thing except the other one just hung down until the wind stream pulled it off and it curled up and took part of the wing with it. The pilot made it back to Tan Son Nhut and come in on emergency, landed on the runway, stopped the aircraft and crawled out, jumped down to the ground and walked away leaving it in the middle of the only runway we have. The RF- 101 guys had to scramble to tow it off the runway because they had the runway shut down.

RF-101

July 13, 1964

They are having an air show up at Da Nang Air Base in the northern part of South Vietnam this weekend

So we have to send one of our aircraft there for display. Plus we have 4 transient unarmed B57Bs from Clark AFB that we were taking care of. They would be carrying to Da Nang the three most important Vietnamese military men in all of Vietnam. They were Major General Khanh, Lt General Ky (Commander of the South Vietnam Air Force) and Brigadier General Tinexx. General Khanh is the big boss over here, he is the Prime Minister of South Vietnam or you could call him the President. They would be flying the B-57Bs to DaNang in formation along with our RB-57E for the air show. I helped send General Khanh off and probably got my picture taken because the place was covered with newspaper reporters. It was quite a deal and all the big wheels were there and here I was right in the middle of them. I got to talk to General Khanh because I helped him strap in the back seat of the B-57B. He asked me how long I have been in his country and where I was from. He could speak excellent English and was extremely friendly. I told him I would be thinking of him at that hot air show on Sunday from the beach in Vung Tau and he said he would rather be with the guys at the beach drinking beer than at the air show but he didn't see it happening any time soon.

Party Time

It's Sunday and the weather is bad at the coast so they cancelled the flight to Vung Tau, but the guys down at work decided to have a party at the pilot's operation building. So everyone gave 50 cents to one of the guys. He went to the BX and bought a fifth of Vodka, 2 fifths of Whisky, a bottle of Gin and a bottle of Scotch. Then the pilots went and bought 15 cases of beer. There were about 20 of us, the pilots, the aircraft ground crew, the camera people, and some of those spooky guys that look at the pictures we take. I never figured out who some of them were till later when I found out who operated the Air America aircraft that would occasionally park in our area, they were from the (CIA) Central Intelligence Agency. Major Musgrove throws a great party and we all were having a great time getting to know each other and feeling great.

Party time 1964 Pilots operation building

Then one of the guys had a motion picture camera and he wanted to get a picture of all of us. So we sat down on a bench but there wasn't room for me so they sat me down on the ground in front of them. Just as the guy started the camera everybody poured there beer or whatever they were drinking right on my head. I had a full glass of Gin and Coke so I threw it over my shoulder and it hit Major McGinnis right in the face, splashed over on two Captains and another Major plus most of the rest of the guys.

They were laughing so hard they didn't know what happened at first, and then I got soaked again. It was those officers that told the rest of the guys to pour their drinks on me, mainly Captain Young. We all had a good time and Sgt Davis had to make sure a couple of our pilots got home to their nice hotels downtown

The next week my airplane went out on a mission and when it came back during the post flight inspection I found a bullet hole in the tail at the very tip of the vertical stabilizer. Major McGinnis and Captain Young were the crew on this mission so I hollered at Major McGinnis as he was leaving the operations building, we got a stand and run it up so we could get a better look. Right away I looked at Major McGinnis and asked him where were you flying my airplane because the bullet entered from the top and come out at a lower point. They were either firing down at you or you were flying my airplane upside down. He explained that their target was in the mountains and they were flying low between them and he knew where it happened and he could see the Viet Cong shooting at them from one of the mountain tops but he didn't think they were hit. We patched the hole and put the aircraft back in service, we did not paint the patch red though.

That same afternoon we had just sent 245 off on a mission and we were cooling off in our air-conditioned trailer. There were 4 of us and I had just sat down with a coke and picked up a news paper. Then all of a sudden there was a huge explosion and the trailer seemed to lift right off the ground. Rocks and dirt was flying everywhere. We all jumped up and started for the door because we thought we had been bombed or hit with mortar fire. Sgt Davis opened the door and all we could see was a big cloud of dust and there was Captain Young standing there with his pistol in his hand right in the middle of this dust cloud. We finally got out of the door and started running for a ditch about 30 yards away, then someone yelled at us to come back. When we turned around we saw what had happened. There was one of those big Cranes; you know the ones with the big tires that stand about 4 ft tall. It was a huge machine that was used to remove crashed aircraft from the runway. Anyway it was coming down the edge of the ramp on the gravel and one of those big tires blew out. When it blew it was about 4 ft from the end of our trailer. It threw gravel and rocks about 20 ft in the air and engulfed our trailer in a big cloud of dust and put 4 or 5 holes in the end of the trailer. It's a good thing someone yelled at us when we were heading for that ditch because I was just about ready to dive into it head first and it was about half full of old stagnant water. Everyone laughed about it afterward even though we were all white as a sheet. It scared the crap out of me and I don't think I have ever been so scared in my life. I just knew we had been hit with mortar fire.

6 F-102 Delta Dagger Interceptors on our flight crowded flight line

Then that afternoon we were working on 245 when a huge C-124 cargo airplane landed and parked near our parking ramp. Then about 10 minutes later, here come six F-102 Delta wing fighter interceptors flying in formation over the airfield. They landed and taxied into our ramp area where their crews parked them at the end toward base operations. When we talked to their guys we found out they are here to stay and they have everything they need in the C-124. They are assigned with protecting the base from air attack. They were fully armed with air to air missiles and rockets.

Our parking ramp is full of airplanes, they are parking them everywhere they can find a solid piece of ground. They even park some of the lighter ones out on the grass between the ramp and the taxiway.

There is every type of airplane you can think of here plus we have a lot of Navy Jets come in here plus British and Australian Jets also. The British sure do make some funny looking aircraft. Not to mention the three or four hundred Huey helicopters, although they park on the grass.

We seem to be having a problem here on the base of running out of room to park aircraft. It's July 28 1964 and 5 KB-50 refueling tankers just arrived. These things are huge, almost as big as a B52; they have 4 propeller engines and 2 Jet engines on them. They will be used to refuel Jet fighters, Air Force and Navy; the Jet engines on them are used to keep up with the fighters during air refueling.

Then base operations called us on the radio that we have in our Metro truck and wanted us to take care of 2 armed B-57Bs from Clark AFB when they landed. We have one of those Metro trucks; you know the ones that look like bread trucks. It is real nice, we have padded benches in it and it has a small fold away table. We sit out there on the flight line at night and play cards while we are waiting on the aircraft to return.

Dealing with an armed aircraft was a first for me and we parked them pointing away toward the taxiway because the guns were hot and very dangerous. When they taxied into our parking area I had to guide them in and those guns were pointed right at me and I did not like it at all. We parked them, refueled them and got them ready to fly again before the guys from Clark arrived here to take care of them. They were then going on to Bien Hoa air base because we don't have room for them here. It's about 30 miles north of here.

July 24, 1965

You don't realize most of the time that there is a war going on here. But when you hear the mortar fire and gun fire it helps.

Monday night we were working on my aircraft 245; it was about 10 pm when all of a sudden we could hear gun fire off in the distance. Then there were flares lighting up the sky just off the end of the runway. Those flares put out about three million candle power of light and when they drop them it's just like its day time. They drop them out of the back of a C-123 from 3000 feet. They have a parachute on them so they come down slow and burn for about 5 minutes. We stopped working and shut off all our lights and proceeded to watch an awesome sight. There were some Viet Cong about 3 miles out at the end of the runway (our end) shooting at the aircraft landing. So the Vietnam Air Force sent up 2 old WW-2 A1-Hs loaded with rockets. They would come right over our heads making their pass and then when they would get lined up they would fire their rockets. They were probably less than half a mile from us and it would light up the sky when they fired, then you would see a huge flash when the rocket hit the ground. Then a second later you would hear the explosion and the whole ground would shake. The pilots that were still at the operations building come out on the flight line with us to see what was going on. Then Captain Young looked up and yelled there were flares coming down on us. Sure enough there were several flares floating down in their parachutes and headed straight for the RF-101s parked on the ramp. The flare was not burning but the canister they were in was red hot. We grabbed some brooms from the office and climbed on those aircraft and directed the canisters away from the aircraft in the dark. With the pilots help we managed to clear every aircraft and direct the canisters to the ground. Anyway the A1s took care of the Viet Cong, they no longer existed and things calmed down.

Then again on Friday night the Viet Cong attacked a small town about five miles from the base and mortar fire shook the barracks all night long. They finished it in the morning when the Vietnamese Air Force sent up three A-1Hs to take care of them.

CHAPTER 3

AUGUST 1964

The War Begins

Sunday August 2 1964

Three North Vietnam P-T boats attacked a US Navy Destroyer patrolling off the coast of North Vietnam. The Navy Destroyer Maddox was attacked with torpedoes and gunfire by three unidentified PT boats in the gulf of Tonkin off North Vietnam. The destroyer was not damaged and there were no injuries to personnel in the un-provoked attack. The PT boats were damaged and driven off by gunfire from 4 F-8 Crusader aircraft from the aircraft carrier Ticonderoga. The Maddox answered with their 5 inch guns. The Navy said that one of the attacking PT boats was badly damaged by Navy aircraft firing Zuni rockets and 20mm machine guns. It was lying dead in the water and the other 2 were retreating slowly due to damage. The attack was in international waters about 80 miles southeast of Hanoi and 30 miles off the coast of North Vietnam.

Tuesday August 4 they did it again, this time there were several North Vietnamese PT boats. They made a second deliberate attack on U.S. ships in international waters off the coast of North Vietnam. A battle raged for about three hours and the U.S. destroyers Maddox and C. Turner Joy sunk two of the communist boats and damaged two others. The Vietnamese PT boats scored no hits on the U.S. ships and there were no injuries to the crewmen. The engagement was fought in bad weather which hampered aircraft from the U.S. aircraft carriers from getting into the fight.

The next day we got into the fight, U.S. Navy planes struck back at the communist attackers, Wednesday and damaged or destroyed approximately 25 North Vietnamese patrol boats at five bases on the coast of North Vietnam. Besides knocking out a large portion of North Vietnam's patrol boat fleet, the U.S. aircraft from the aircraft carriers Ticonderoga and Constellation blew up an oil depot and other base facilities. The low level air attacks were carried out over a period of about 5 hours.

Two Navy aircraft were shot down by antiaircraft fire from ground batteries. The pilots were presumed lost. One other plane was slightly damaged. The base here in Saigon was put on alert and I had to get to my duty station as quick as possible. When I got to work we sent both of our aircraft off to go to North Vietnam plus most of the RF-101s to take pictures and the F-102s to fly cover to protect them. The Navy and the Air Force were attacking the North Vietnam PT boat bases so we sent our aircraft to take pictures at low levels to check the damage. The RF-101s will take high altitude pictures and we will come in at low altitude and get high resolution pictures. The F-102s will fly cover to make sure North Vietnam doesn't send up any aircraft against our unarmed aircraft. The results of the reconnaissance flights were very successful and confirmed initial pilot reports of success. We got some exceptional High definition pictures of the damage to their bases and our pilots reported no antiaircraft fire, such as that which shot down the two Navy aircraft earlier.

Things seem to be moving really fast here, an aircraft carrier task group is being shifted from the First Fleet, which operates off the U.S. Pacific coast, to the western Pacific. The attack group is normally based at San Diego. F-102 Delta Dagger Interceptors and B-57B Fighter Bombers from Clark A.F.B. have been moved into South Vietnam. This makes me very happy because now we can ward off any North Vietnamese air attack on South Vietnam with the F-102s and counter-attack with B-57B fighter bombers against enemy bases.

To top it all off 30 B-57B fighter bombers were being transferred from Clark AFB under cover of darkness to Bien Hoa airfield 20 miles north of here. One of the bombers crashed in Viet Cong controlled territory 10 miles east of the Bien Hoa airfield. They were on final approach to the runway when they; for some reason crashed into the jungle. Search planes said they saw no survivors and ground parties could not enter the area because of strong Viet Cong fire. Two other B-57Bs crashed together on the runway at Bien Hoa airfield during landing at the same time. No casualties were reported in those accidents but they blocked the runway. There were still 5 aircraft in the air and the runway was blocked so they were diverted to Saigon. Base operations called me and said we would have to take care of them because Transient alert was busy with all the other aircraft that were being diverted from Bien Hoa. There was only one problem; there was only Sgt Ware and myself working that night. So we went over to our pilots operation building; only Major Musgrove and Major Mc Guinness were there so we commandeered them and one of the RF-101 mechanics to help us. Then operations called and said the aircraft were 'HOT" which means they were fully armed, guns and this time a half a dozen 250lb bombs hanging under the wings. Guns we could handle but bombs were another story so Major Musgrove went over and talked to the F-102 troops and they sent one of their armament guys to make sure the aircraft were safe after we get them parked. I sure didn't want one of those bombs falling off an airplane on the parking ramp. Because it was late at night all we had to do was find a place to park them and get the crews over to our 5 star hotels, (tent city) their troops would be over in the morning to take care of them. We found a place to park them and safely put the aircraft and the crews to bed. The next day Major Musgrove took 243 up and took pictures of the downed B-57, the canopy was still closed so the pilots did not survive and he said they were shooting at him as he made some low passes over the airplane. We checked 243 over real good and found they missed him. I talked to Major Musgrove and told him I hung out with some of the B-57B mechanics on my way over here and asked him if he knew what happened, why they just flew into the ground. He speculated that the problem might have been these guys have been training at Clark AFB on the bombing range. The B-57 handles quite different with bombs hanging out under the wings and they would take off with the bombs then drop them on the range. They did not practice very much on landing with them which in this case they had to do and it is quite difficult. Probably they lost too much air speed and stalled the aircraft and crashed into the jungle. Anyway the B-57Bs are here from Clark AFB and I feel just a little bit safer.

We had a very eventful week so Major Musgrove decided we would have a party Saturday afternoon. We had sent 245 over to Clark AFB for its 100 hr inspection on Friday and 243 was only flying in the morning so Saturday would work out just fine. Plus we will be losing 3 of our guys in a few days so this party will be for them also.

This is going to be a big one. All the airmen from the camera section and the maintenance section which I am the only airman in the maintenance section had to give $1.50, there were 8 of us. All the NCOs from both sections had to contribute $3.00 and all the officers pitched in $8.00. We collected about $125.00. Major Musgrove went to the chow hall and got 50 New York strip steaks from the chow hall commander, he gave them to us only if he could join the party. Plus he would bring a bunch of other things to go with them. Including the bar-b-que equipment to cook them over an open fire, (a 55 gal drum cut in half and charcoal.) He was a great guy and attended most of our monthly parties.

The money was used to buy all kinds of booze and The Major hired a Vietnamese cook and a bartender. Just in case we have to fly 243 in the afternoon we had to have one flight crew and one mechanic not to partake of any booze, Sgt Ware drew the short straw even though they tried to make me do it because I am the lowest in rank. Thank you Sgt Cogdill for sticking up for me. It was a great time and well worth my investment, we went all out on this one and it took our minds off the war for awhile.

One of our monthly parties

More Party

Then Major Stanfield was having a drink and looking out onto the flight line at the 5 B-57B aircraft with the bombs hanging under the wings. He looked at me and asked if the 20 millimeter guns were loaded and I told him yes that they were. He then said that he had seen one time back in the States static electricity had set them off. That stopped our party in its tracks and everybody moved out of the way of those gun sights. We then grabbed a tractor tug and turned each of them to point out over the taxiway. We were glad to see them leave for Bien Hoa later that afternoon.

Chinese Jets in North Vietnam

Monday morning Aug 10th 1964

Major Musgrove called in all of us in the RB-57E to attend a top secret briefing that only the pilots usually had. Saturday morning 243s mission was to take pictures over a North Vietnam military base. They came in low under the North Vietnam radar and then high tailed it out of there. They showed us a picture 243 took of the air base that has 32 Mig 15 and Mig 17 jet fighters on it from Red China. They are sub sonic jet fighters similar to our F-86 fighters from the Korean War era.

Understandably our pilots were not very happy about this news. Because of this, the U.S. defense department sent 60 F-100 jet fighters into South Vietnam. Most of them went to Da Nang Air Base about 60 miles south of the North Vietnam border. We had to find a place to put 10 of them on our congested flight line but we were happy to do so. During the Korean War our F-86 fighters were knocking down 12 Migs to our 1 F-86. So you can figure if they sent all 32 of them at us we would only need 10 or less F-100s to take them out.

The F-100 is slow compared to the six supersonic F-102s we have here and six more at Da Nang Air Base. Plus we have supersonic F-105s stationed in Thailand and F-8s and the new F-4s on the Navy carriers just off North Vietnam. They never did send those Migs south of the border. Although our pilots told us about a Mig 15 that did fly close to the border trying to shoot down a South Vietnamese A-1H Sky Rader. The A-1H aircraft returned the attack and hit the Mig 15 and it was smoking when it disappeared into a cloud claiming the first possible kill of a Mig in the war. An American pilot was flying the old WW-2 A1-H South Vietnam fighter bomber.

The next day Sgt Cogdill announced that my aircraft 245 would be returning to General Dynamics in Fort Worth Texas for modifications in a few days. They are going to install new radar in it like that in a hound dog missile that the B-52 bomber carries under the wings. With this radar the pilot can take off and turn it on and take a nap if he wanted to. The aircraft will fly at whatever altitude the pilot sets into it, if they come up on a mountain the airplane will climb up over it at whatever the set altitude is. It will help them out quite a bit, there are a lot of mountains up north of here and if they are flying in bad weather using the infrared they won't have to worry about hitting one. Plus if they go into North Vietnam they can go down to 500ft, under the North Vietnam radar and turn it on and the airplane will stay at that altitude. Even if they come up on a big hill they will climb up over it and clear it by exactly 500ft. All they will have to do is take pictures and not worry about flying the aircraft. Major Stanfield and Lt.Platt will be flying it back to the States, the lucky dogs. The 3 Majors flipped coins to see who would fly it back and the odd man wins which were Major Stanfield and his navigator Lt. Platt. I tried to convince them that the crew chief should go too and they agreed except there are only 2 seats and Major Stanfield wouldn't leave Lt. Platt because I didn't know how to navigate. I guess that was a good reason. They will fly over to Clark AFB where they will remove the cameras from the bomb bay and install a ferry tank. They will need the extra fuel to make it across the ocean; they couldn't make it without that extra fuel. They will fly from Clark to Guam to Wake Island to Hickam field in Hawaii to Travis AFB San Francisco then To Fort Worth, Texas. They will be gone about 2 months then back the same way.

Because we will have only one airplane (243), they moved Sgt. Gibson and Sgt Gilmore to transient alert until they leave later this month, now we have only 4 guys. Plus they cut out all day flying for the RB-57s. The RF-101s are going to take all the day targets and we will take the night targets because we have the Infra- Red cameras and photo flash. Also Sgt Cogdill put 3 of us on night shift and he will work days by himself. What a deal! Because we will take turns on having a night off every 3rd night, otherwise work 2 nights then a night off. So if they should fly during the day whoever was off the night before would come in and help Sgt Gogdill get the aircraft ready.

Thursday morning I was over at the airman's club with Davis drinking coffee when all of a sudden there was this big explosion that shook the whole club and broke some of the windows. Everyone jumped up and ran outside but there was no explosion. Then I realized what had happened because I had heard it before. They were announcing on Armed Forces Radio that a F-102 had broke the sound barrier over Saigon and that steps were being taken so it wouldn't happen again. They said everyone in Saigon was heading for the bomb shelters. I sure wouldn't want to be the pilot of that aircraft he is going to get a good chewing out. He scared all of us half to death but the base commander later thought it was funny.

They are hard to see 96 Huey helicopters parked across the runway in the distance

Ninety Six Huey Helicopters

Later that afternoon when I arrived at work at 4:30 I looked out across the runway and there were about 100 Huey helicopters sitting in the grass loading South Vietnamese troops. Then they all started their jet engines and took off. Have you ever seen a swarm of bees? Well that's what it looked like there were so many. I don't know how they kept from running into each other; the sky was black with them.

Intelligence reports and Ariel photos from our aircraft indicated between 2000 and 3000 Viet Cong had massed for a strike about 30 miles north of Saigon. Therefore 96 Huey helicopters one of the largest helicopter assaults of the Republic of Vietnam's war was hurled into the jungle carrying close to 1000 Vietnamese troops. It was a cleanup operation and they did clean up big time.

When they come back from unloading all those troops you could see them off in the distance flying in formation, WOW, Ninety-six Huey helicopters both Vietnamese and U.S. Army, the sky was full of them. Everywhere you look all you could see was helicopters. Then when they got close to the base they went into single file that looked like a great long train in the sky. That was quite a sight to see all those Huey's in the air at one time.

Friday Aug 14 1964

Radar picked up an unidentified aircraft heading toward Saigon. Four F-102s scrambled to intercept it and check it out. It turned out to be an Australian Canberra jet fighter bomber that was off course, I bet those Limeys had the crap scared out of them when they saw those F-102s coming after them. Their Canberra is the same as our B-57 Canberra except it has Rolls Royce engines and the cockpit is different and has four crew members instead of two like ours. It was pretty neat to see the F-102s and that Aussy jet come over the base flying in formation. Transient alert parked them near our area and an hour or so later the pilot came out to our aircraft and said he had a little problem. He said that after they landed he ordered a fuel truck and a Shell truck come out and they filled his #1 and #2 fuel tanks with JP-1 fuel (Jet petroleum #1) and he wanted to know if I thought it would be ok to fly it with that fuel. We aren't supposed to use anything but JP-4 fuel in our engines. I really didn't know what to tell him so I called Sgt Cogdill out and Sgt Cogdill immediately ordered the tanks be pumped of that fuel and refilled with JP-4. They were headed up north to Da Nang Air Base about 60 miles from North Vietnam, although they would be back to Saigon every month or so. Our pilots became good friends with them and they hung out with them whenever they were in town.

That afternoon Sgt Ware and I sent Major McGinnis and Captain Young off on a mission in 243. We watched them take off and then put all our equipment away and we headed to the trailer to cool off. Then we saw all the fire trucks going out to the runway with their red lights flashing. So we decided we would go out and see what was coming in on emergency. This happened quite often and everybody would stop what they were doing and go see if the aircraft would make it or crash on the runway. The next thing we see is 243 coming in on emergency with the left engine shut down and smoking. When they were on the ground the engine quit smoking so they taxied in on one engine with the fire trucks behind them. Major McGinnis said soon after they were in the air the #1 engine started to vibrate violently so he shut it down. He had to land the aircraft that was full of fuel on one engine; this is extremely hard and dangerous. So we removed the engine nose cowling and found the #1 generator had literally disintegrated and that was causing the problem. We installed a new generator then run the engine to make sure it is working with no engine vibration. The aircraft has four generators, two on each engine and they have to be adjusted to put out exactly the same voltage (28Volts). Then we had to reinstall the engine nose cowling which is the hardest part of the job, it took us two hours to get it back on. If you are reading this and worked on the B-57 you know what I am talking about. By the time we fueled and completed the post flight inspection of the aircraft it was 2am in the morning.

That same night around 10pm, while we were changing that generator on 243 the air attack siren went off. They scrambled 3 F-102s, they all 3 started their engines at the same time. But one of them shut down his engine because there was something wrong with the aircraft. So the other 2 taxied out and took off. It took 3 minutes to get them in the air from the time the horn blew. The pilot that shut down his aircraft jumped out of that one and run over to the standby aircraft and jumps into it. He tries to start the engine but this one wouldn't even start, so he gave up and went back to bed I guess. It's a good thing it was just a practice scramble.

Our night off

Sgt Gogdill said the next day that we did such a good job getting 243 back in flying condition that Sgt Ware and I could take the night off and he would come in and take our place. Major Musgrove was so happy with Sgt Ware and me, he came out on the flight line and handed Sgt Ware a 5 dollar bill and said for us to have a good time on our night off.

So we did, we started off at the airman's club that afternoon. Let me tell you about the clubs we have here on the base. We have an Officer's club, a NCO club and an Airman's club; normally they are rated in that order. But here at Tan Son Nhut it is just the opposite, the Airman's club is the best then the NCO club and the Officers club is last. The Airman's club makes the most money, has the best bands and is 10 times better looking inside than either of the other clubs. If you are not a member you can only get in if you are a members guest. So when we have a band at the Airman's club the pilots and the NCO's want me to take them with me. Sgt Ware and I started out at the Airman's club then decided we would go to Saigon for dinner. We caught the bus to town and got off downtown at the Tu Do Street stop. We took the 5 dollars Major Musgrove gave us and changed it to Vietnamese Peastras on the black market. This gave us enough money to have a great dinner, drink all night and still have taxi fare to get back to the base.

We started out at the My Canh floating restaurant where we ate a great steak dinner. The My Canh floating restaurant was very popular and was highly recommended by our pilots. It is built on a large barge floating on the Saigon River near the end of Tu Do Street downtown. The restaurant was very plush inside and had an outside dining area overlooking the Saigon River and had the best food in town and was safe to eat. On June 25 1965 shortly after I left Vietnam it was blown up by the Viet Cong killing 41 and injuring 81 men woman and children. I guess it wasn't so safe after all.

Jet Fighter Races

After dinner we hit a couple of bars in Saigon then caught a taxi to Cholon. The Army operates a hotel there and they have a great bar and it is safe. When we entered the bar there were a couple of our Pilots there, sitting with some other guys. They saw us and hollered for us to come join them and they would buy us a drink. We sat down with them at their table and ordered our drinks. The other guys with them were an F-102 pilot and two RF-101 pilots. They were telling them how great we were because we got 243 back in flying condition so fast. If he only knew the things we said to that nose cone we had so much trouble with. They continued their conversation that they had been talking about. It seems the F-102s and the F-101s have been having Jet Fighter races on takeoff. They would line up on the runway in formation then hit their afterburners and take off side by side and the first one that gets to 10,000 feet wins and the loser buys the drinks. The F-102 pilot was buying the drinks, (ours included) and complaining that the RF-101 hit his afterburners before he did and that is why he lost big time and he wants a rematch. About this time the two guys sitting at the next table slid their chairs over and wondered if they could get in on the conversation. They were Navy F-8 Crusader pilots from the aircraft carrier Ticonderoga. They had been part of the bunch that attacked the North Vietnamese PT Boat bases back in August. They said they were on a routine patrol mission yesterday protecting the fleet and they couldn't get back to the Carrier because of bad weather. They had their choice, they could divert to Da Nang Air Base or Tan Son Nhut in Saigon. They understandably chose to spend the weekend in Saigon and they were staying there at the hotel. They said their F-8 aircraft was faster than anything around and could easily beat either the F-102 or the F-101. Wow, that really got the conversation going and Sgt Ware finally said there was only one way to find out for sure and everybody agreed. The F-8 pilots said the weather was supposed to clear over the Carrier on Tuesday and they would be leaving around 3pm and we could settle it then. We all had a great time that night and made two good friends from the carrier Ticonderoga that we did see again.

Air Force F-102 Delta Dagger

On Monday they all got together and set up the Jet Fighter races for the next day when the F-8s were leaving. The biggest problem was the fighting among the F-102 and the RF-101 pilots on who was going to kick the Navy's butt and fly in the races. Not to mention the crew chiefs who wanted their aircraft to race. The word got around all over the base and quite a crowd turned out on the flight line to watch. Tuesday afternoon Sgt Ware and I even went to work early so we could watch.

Navy F-8 Crusader

That afternoon two Navy F-8 Crusaders One Air Force RF-101 Voo Doo and one Air Force F-102 Delta Dagger taxied out to the west end of the runway together. We are located at the east end of the runway and I climbed up onto the tail of 245 to get a good view.

Air Force RF-101 Voo Doo

First up were a RF-101 Voo Doo and one of the F-8 Crusaders, it was the first time I have ever seen the Navy and the Air Force make a formation takeoff. We didn't think the F-8 had much of a chance because it only has one J-57 jet engine with afterburner and the RF-101 has two J-57 jet engines with afterburners. They lined up on the runway and started their take off roll, then hit their afterburners at the same time. Of course the RF-101 got way out ahead of the F-8 but the F-8 is much lighter than the RF-101 and he left the ground way before the RF-101. The RF-101 was about a quarter of a mile ahead when he lifted off the ground and retracted his landing gear, they both stayed low to the runway all the way until the RF-101 was about even with us. Then he pulled back on the stick and went straight up with both afterburners still going then the F-8 went straight up right behind the RF-101 afterburner firing. The last we saw of them was when they went through the clouds at about 10,000 ft still going straight up with the RF-101 way ahead.

Next up were the F-102 Delta Dagger and the other F-8 Crusader, they started their takeoff roll and both hit their afterburners at the same time. This was a more equal race because they both have J-57 engines with afterburners and about the same weight with the F-8 slightly lower.

When they came by us they were side by side, then they also went straight up and when they went through the clouds they were still neck and neck. When the F-102 pilot landed back at Tan Son Nhut he said the F-8 beat him through 10,000ft by less than 3 seconds. Then about 5 or 10 minutes later here they come over the base flying in formation what a sight to see 2 Navy F8s, an Air Force F-102 and a RF-101 in formation. The F-102 and the RF-101 peeled off and landed and the Navy F-8s headed out to the Ticonderoga Carrier in the gulf of Tonkin.

After that the RF-101 pilots were after the Navy to bring over one of those new McDonald Douglas F-4 Phantom fighters, they didn't think anything could beat them. I don't know if that ever happened or not but that would be a good race. The F-4 has two more powerful J-79 engines with afterburners but is heavier than the F-101.

The next day we got bad news, they cancelled 245 from going to Fort Worth. Major Stanfield and Lt Platt sure were downhearted, they were so looking forward to that trip and be home with their family for a few weeks. Plus it makes a lot more work for Sgt Cogdill, Sgt Ware and Me as we are the only ones left.

Starting the first of September Tech Sgt Wetzell from transient alert is coming to help us until we can get more replacements so that will help. In the meantime we will have to handle two night flights each night for the next week. Sgt Wetzell, Sgt Ware and I will work nights and Sgt Cogdill will stay on days. That was fine with me because I like the night shift, its cooler at night and I don't have to worry about getting up in the morning.

That same day a brand new French passenger Jet taxied up to the Air Vietnam area. The Air Vietnam hangers are located next to our flight line. It's a French aircraft called the Caravel; it's a nice looking airplane and has two jet engines on the tail. It will be interesting to see if they haul chickens and pigs along with the people, like they do in the old C-47s they have.

Wednesday August 24, 1964

We were getting 243 ready for a four o'clock take off when the fire trucks went screaming out to the runway. Then three A1-H South Vietnamese Fighter Bombers flew over the field in formation. They all had their landing gear lowered except for one of them, then they came back over the base in formation and we could see that one of them had major damage to the underside of the aircraft. There was so much damage that neither main landing gear would come down and pieces of metal were flopping in the breeze and every now and then a piece would fly off. The other two A1's peeled off and come in and landed from our end of the runway with no problems. Then they foamed the runway starting straight out from where we were watching and toward the west end of the runway, approximately 100 yards long. Then we could see the damaged airplane coming in toward the runway and off in the distance, he was going real slow and just hanging in the air. Sgt. Cogdill said he didn't like it that he was going so slow, the aircraft was wandering all over the place and he said he is going to stall out if he doesn't speed up, we need to pray for him. About the time Sgt. Cogdill started praying for him he stalled out and the aircraft come down and hit the ground about 50 yards from the end of the runway, skidded along the ground and onto the runway. The propeller hit the ground and pieces of the aircraft were flying all over the place.

When he hit the foam the aircraft was swapping ends going around and around and 20 millimeter live ammo was coming out of the aircraft and was flying all over the place, even on to the taxiway right in front of us. The aircraft was coming apart and then skidded off the runway, nosed over onto its top and stopped upside down and caught fire. The fire trucks quickly put out the fire and we could see the Pilot crawl out from under the aircraft and run into the arms of one of the firemen. I looked over at Sgt Cogdill and said it's a good thing you prayed for that Pilot, it looks like he is going to make it. What a mess, live ammo all over the runway, in the grass and on the taxiway, parts and pieces everywhere. It only took them 30 minutes to reopen the runway then Big Mo (that's what we call that big machine that blew its tire next to our trailer) picked up what was left of the A1-H and hauled it off to the junk yard.

Thursday August 25, 1964

A General Dynamics test pilot from Fort Worth showed up. He held the rank of Captain and started flying missions with our guys. They are going to modify 3 or 4 more B-57E models into RB-57E (Patricia Lynn) models. He flew several times as the pilot to see how the aircraft handled and he flew the back seat and took the pictures to see how our system worked.

He was extremely impressed with our operation and said we would have more aircraft soon and they are working on them now. We told him they better send some help with them because we have all we can do with the two aircraft we have. Plus he said they still may send 245 back to install radar in it and upgrade the cameras, but right now it is needed here. Also the last mission he flew in the back seat of 243 they were hit three times in the tail with small arms fire. When they landed he said OK' that's enough I can go home now and tell everyone I was almost shot down in Vietnam.

At the end of that week the Generals that were running things over here called Major Musgrove to a meeting. They wanted one of our aircraft in the air all the time during the hours of dark using our Infra-Red cameras. They told him that our air intelligence was providing such important information using the Infra-Red cameras that they wanted us to fly all night. Major Musgrove told them it couldn't be done with just two aircraft. He said if he had ten aircraft and thirty mechanics he could do it. As it is we are flying the two aircraft each night. They relented and told Major Musgrove that we would be getting help soon and they were extremely impressed with the job we are doing.

CHAPTER 4

SEPTEMBER 1964

Student Unrest

September 3, 1964

Last week there were 3,000 Vietnamese students demonstrating just outside the main gate. Our barracks is only about 300 yards from the gate and there were several of us watching from the upper entrance near my bunk. We could see the whole show from up there and we all thought it was funny until they started pushing their way through the gate. They turned loose on them with fire hoses from 3 fire trucks they had out there, plus they were firing machine guns over their heads. That convinced them they didn't really want to get on the base. After all that, they had a helicopter drop leaflets over them and they left and went downtown to do their demonstrating. I don't know what the leaflets said but it seemed to do the trick. There have been a lot of problems recently with the students, so much so that we are restricted to the base. They seem to have some kind of problem with the government.

Here is a part of the whitepaper compiled by South Vietnamese and the American military that I quoted in the first part of this book.

The student population of South Vietnam is an important target group for Viet Cong propagandists. These agents seek to win adherence for the Communist cause among young workers, students in high school, universities and the younger officers and enlisted men in the Armed Forces of the Republic of South Vietnam.

Typical of the agents sent into South Vietnam for this purpose is Nguyen Van Vy a 19-year-old Viet Cong propagandist. He is a native of the Vimh

Linh district of North Vietnam, just north of the demilitarized zone. He was a member of the communist party youth group in his native village. He was recruited for Propaganda work in the South in the fall of 1962. He was one of 40 young people enrolled in a special training course given by the Communist Party in his district. The first phase of the training consisted of political indoctrination. Those who successfully completed the first phase were selected for the second level of training the so-called technical training phase. Then the trainees were given their mission in the South. Vy was told he should infiltrate into South Vietnam and their surrender to the authorities, describing himself as a defector "who was tired of the miserable life in the North". He was to say he wanted to complete his schooling which was impossible in the North. He was told to ask to live with relatives in the South so he could go to school. Once his story was accepted and he was enrolled in a school, he was to begin his work propagandadizing other students.

He was assigned to work under an older agent to whom he had to report regularly, the third member of the team was a younger man who was to assist Vy. The three were to infiltrate into South Vietnam separately and to meet there at a rendezvous point. At first Vy was to do no more than to observe his fellow students carefully, collecting biographical data on them and studying their personalities and capabilities. He was then to select those he thought might be most influenced by communist propaganda and try to make friends with them. Vy entered South Vietnam on June 2, 1963, by swimming across the Ben Hai River. He encountered an elderly farmer who led him to the local authorities, there he told his story but it was not believed. He then admitted his true mission. This is how the North Vietnamese agents infiltrated the student population in South Vietnam.

The next week the students were back this time there were more of them. They stormed the main gate and even though the fire hoses were pushing them back, 6 of them broke loose and were running down the road into the base. The South Vietnamese opened fire on them with 50cal machine guns and killed them all. I am glad I was working when that happened, that would have been scary. After that they declared martial law and arrested over 100 of them, they were all Viet Cong. This seemed to quiet them down at least for the time being. When they had the funeral for the 6 dead students there were 30,000 people in the procession. After things calmed down they lifted the restrictions on going to Saigon but you have to be off the streets after midnight. They were extremely strict about that, our military police, the Quan Kahn, (Vietnamese military police) and the Saigon police; we called the latter (White Mice) because they dressed in all white uniforms. They could and would shoot anyone they find on the streets.

Saigon has a large Olympic size swimming pool and it was closed in March of 1964 because it was falling apart. The Navy got a hold of it and is in the process of remodeling it. I have never seen such a big pool in my life. It is an Olympic swimming pool that the French built when they were here back in the fifties. It is 75 yards long and 30 yards wide, it has a balcony with a nice snack bar on the upper level. There are nice lounge chairs and at one end they have ping pong tables. It is a beautiful pool and is entirely made out of tiles. There is a 50ft diving platform and a 30 ft platform but they are understandably closed off. There is a 20ft diving board and two 15ft diving boards plus two 6ft diving boards. The diving boards are built like a pyramid and the water is from 3ft deep to 28ft deep. It is open every day from 10am till 8pm at night. The pool is lighted under water and there are lights all around the balcony. There is a bomb screen all around the outside of the building and several guards. Only Americans and Diplomats and their familys are allowed to swim there. It was a nice place to go and it was safe plus every now and then Navy Nurses would show up which was nice. I spent many hours there during the year I was in Vietnam.

Saigon pool

September 5, 1964

Six more F-102s arrived, now we have 12 armed and ready to go. Major Musgrove told us that the Generals wanted the RB-57E aircraft 55-4244 that is in Fort Worth over here. I guess they then decided not to bring it over here because they use that aircraft to train the flight crews and more aircraft are being modified so it will be needed there.

On Tuesday September 8, 1964 three new men arrived, all three of them are from Japan on a 120 day temporary duty. Sgt Cogdill said he would train them on the day shift and they would get both aircraft ready to fly each day. Sgt Ware and I would then come in and get both aircraft into the air and take care of them when they return. Sgt Wetzell would go back to transient alert. This worked out pretty good except we later found out their orders were messed up. All 3 of them have F-102 experience and if they find out they messed up their orders they will probably take them and put them with the F-102s. But for now we have them and they love the RB-57E compared to the complicated F-102.

We never did tell the F-102 people and our guys didn't say anything either so we got to keep them the whole 120 days.

Two days later another new guy showed up, Airman First Class Chuck Burton and this time he wasn't temporary we get him for a full year. Sgt Cogdill put him on the night shift with Sgt Ware and me for us to train him. The problem was that he already had two years experience on the B-57 so he ended up training us. Chuck and I became best friends, we had a lot in common we were the same age and both of us got married about the same time. Most of the Air Force men that were sent to Vietnam during the early years of the war were married; I guess they figured we were more stable although it was harder on us than the single guys.

Saturday September 12th

We had just sent off both our aircraft on a mission and we were on our way to the chow hall for dinner. Just as we passed in front of the F-102s 4 of them almost run over us as they scrambled. This time it was not a practice, Vietnamese Air Force commander, Air Commodore; Nguyen Cao Ky ordered the F-102s sent aloft after a Cambodian Soviet-made Mig-17 jet fighter attacked two of his A-1H propeller driven fighter bombers. The A-1s were flying air cover over a border region where Vietnamese and Cambodian soldiers were fighting a land, air and river battle when they were attacked by a Cambodian Mig. This was the first time the F-102s were scrambled against a Mig in the Vietnam War. The U. S. jets were armed with their regular air to air missiles. The F-102s set up a protective air umbrella cover over the battle zone, while Vietnamese A-1H Sky Raider fighter bombers, bombed and strafed Cambodia river boats which had crossed the border to shell a Vietnamese outpost. The Mig's high tailed it out of there before the F-102s showed up because they didn't want to deal with the F-102s radar controlled heat seeking missiles.

Vietnamese ministry spokesmen said the engagement opened when Cambodian border guards poured mortar and recoilless cannon fire into a Vietnamese Army unit in order to help a band of about 30 Viet Cong escape into Cambodia. The F-102 pilots told us they had orders to stay in Vietnamese air space and to fire only in self- defense which to them meant shoot down any Mig-17 they could see wherever it happened to be. General Ky said as many as 6 of his A-1H Sky Raiders were in action under the umbrella at one time The F-102 pilots said they were amazed watching the A-1s at what they could do.

As soon as we got back from dinner we see the Fire trucks were scrambled for an aircraft coming in on emergency, then base operations called and said 245 was in trouble. Major McGuiness said he had an unsafe landing gear indicator and didn't know if the landing gear was down and locked or not. The indicator light that told him when the gear is up and locked or down and locked was coming on and off. He flew over the tower and they told him the gear looked OK to them. He landed without any problems and Chuck Burton said to order a new indicator micro switch for the nose landing gear. When Major McGuiness parked and opened the canopy the first thing he said was to check the nose gear indicator switch because he has had this problem before. So Sgt Ware ordered the switch and we had to haul out the jacks and jack up the aircraft. We had to drag out the hydraulic power equipment to hook to the airplane so we can run the landing gear up and down. Sure enough Chuck and the Major were right the switch was bad. Plus Sgt Ware decided that while we had the aircraft on jacks we might as well go ahead and change the two nose tires because they were getting worn. There is where we run into all our trouble, because they have been on that aircraft a long time so they didn't want to come off. We kicked them beat them and cussed them for over an hour and they wouldn't budge, then I went and found a big iron pipe and finally convinced them to come off. We didn't get out of there till 3am the next morning.

September 12, 1964

We had a lighting unit out at the aircraft while we were working and it lit up the whole area. In South Vietnam they have these big ole bugs called rice bugs (all they eat is rice) and they were attracted to the lights. They are big bugs some about the size of your hand and it hurts if they fly into you. Big ole things and they look mean like they might bite you. When they get ready to fly they pump back and forth then take off like they have afterburners and you better be out of the way. When I went up to the Esso fuel office to get a fuel truck to top off the aircraft I told the Vietnamese truck driver that a bunch of rice bugs were all over the place around the aircraft. Wow, he and another guy grabbed their hats and a couple of buckets, jumped in the fuel truck and beat me back to the aircraft with that big truck. They picked up around 200 of those big bugs and put them in the big buckets they brought. We asked them what they were going to do with them, they said (number one chop-chop) which means they were going to take them home and eat them. They ate some of them right there on the spot and I thought Chuck was going to hurl. They would get the ones that were about the size of your hand would turn them over on their backs, grab them under their throats, rip them open and eat the guts and everything out of them. They tried to get us to help pick them up but I wasn't about to touch one of those ugly things. You couldn't even walk around the aircraft without hearing a "crunch" under your feet when you stepped on one of those big ole things.

Coup d'état

Sunday September 13 1964

Four battalions of South Vietnamese troops moved into Saigon, spearheaded by armored units and led by Interior Minister General Lam Van Phat and

Saigon mayor Doung Ngoe Lam. Both had been fired last week by Prime Minister General Nguyen Khanh. The rebel troops invaded Khanh's office and arrested several duty officers but found no trace of General Khanh. The local radio station reported he had escaped to Tan Son Nhut airbase earlier. The rebels also occupied the communications centers in Saigon. They seized the Central Post Office and the government radio station plus they disarmed police posts all over town at gun point. Phat appeared to be in complete control of the situation. With him were the commander of the Vietnamese Army IV corps, General Due and several officers that had also been fired by General Khanh. Rebel headquarters were set up at the home of the former Mayor of Saigon.

We had been hearing reports all morning and afternoon on what was happening on the radio and the base was closed and we were restricted to the base. When we arrived at work on the flight line we were ordered to stay at work until further notice. Before I left the barracks which is close to the main gate I noticed the gate was closed and several South Vietnamese tanks had gathered outside the gate and they were demanding that General Ky, the Vietnam Air Force commander surrender the base. About 30 minutes after we arrived at work we were getting my aircraft ready to fly and when I looked up here come a tank rumbling down the flight line. The tank commander stopped his tank right in front of the F-102s and got out. Major Musgrove walked over to him and asked him what he is doing on our flight line. He spoke good English and told Major Musgrove not to worry they were just having a little political problem and everything will be Ok. Just then here comes a Vietnam Air Force A-1H Sky raider going about 300 miles per hour 100 feet above the ground right down the flight line over the tank, he pulled up, turned around and came back. The tank commander got back in the tank and the guy manning the 50cal machine gun on the tank followed the A-1 on each of his several passes. We thought for sure he was going to fire at the A-1 but he never did. Evidently this tank had got on the base through the civilian terminal before they closed it. He parked it in front of the F-102s because he figured they would not fire on him parked so close to them. The tank commander told Major Musgrove that he wasn't sure he supported the rebels but he was obeying his orders so far. We decided the safest place for us is right where we are and about an hour later the tank left the base. Then more A-1s showed up from other bases in Vietnam there must have been 25 or 30 of them, they landed and parked over near the civilian air terminal. In radio broadcasts the rebels claimed the support of the entire South Vietnamese military.

But one commander ignored the broadcast which said he had sided with the rebels. He was the commander of Vietnams new Air Force; Air Commodore 34 year old Nguyen Cao Ky. (our hero) Ky had gone on record saying he is opposed to all coups. General Ky is an amazing man; he can fly just about every aircraft we have over here and is absolutely loved by his fellow pilots and all of us Americans.

Singlehandedly General Ky rallied all the units in the country which were still loyal to the government. He sent up a squadron of A-1E Sky Rader fighter bombers loaded with rockets, bombs and napalm bombs.

They flew menacing passes over the rebel troops in Saigon and around Tan Son Nhut airfield. General Ky communicated with them through his command Jeep which had the only radio capable of reaching them. He called the rebels by phone from his office at Tan Son Nhut and told them he was prepared to hold Tan Son Nhut by force and he had the support of the Navy, Marines, Paratroopers and the Army First Corps.

Meanwhile Prime minster General Nguyen Khnah left Tan Son Nhut for the safety of the seaside resort of Cap St Jacques where he will run the country from there. Before he left he told General Ky he was free to deal with the rebels as he saw fit but to avoid fighting if possible. General Ky told him they were in a position to destroy the rebels but he thought he could settle this without force.

That night we were restricted to the flight line and it was a good thing because they dropped flares over the base all night. We were running all over the place chasing those hot canisters coming down with their parachutes and trying to keep them from landing on all the aircraft on the flight line. Then about 11pm base supply sent 22 M2 Automatic Rifles and 22 45cal pistols with 5000 rounds of ammunition for everybody in the recon section. That got all of our attention that maybe this might be more serious than we thought.

The next day General Ky ordered a C-47 transport aircraft airborne to act as a relay for radio contact with the loyal officers in the South Vietnamese military that were supporting General Khanh and him.

Then Deputy U.S. Ambassador Alexis Johnson met with General Due, one of the rebel leaders and General Due assured him that the American troops on the base were safe, this was nice to hear. Then Prime Minister Khanh returned to Tan Son Nhut to meet with General Ky and Ambassador Johnson. Ambassador Johnson told them that he attempted to dissuade the rebels from the coup attempt and reported that the rebel's morale had fallen sharply after several units reverted to government control.

By this time General Ky had lost contact with the rebels so he sent a message with a news reporter to rebel leader General Due for him to call him at his office on Tan Son Nhut airfield.

Within an hour General Due called Ky and told him there would be no fighting in the capital and the rebels were going back to the delta to fight the Viet Cong, the coup was over.

General Ky told General Due that he understood his complaints and they agreed to discuss Due's differences with the government at Tan Son Nhut the next morning.

Premier General Nguyen Khanh survived Sunday's coup but Monday faced the danger of another coup from his loyal young officers unless their demands are met.

We heard on the radio that when Premier Khanh returned to his office in Saigon late Monday he was presented a three-point demand from the loyalist officers who had saved his American backed government from armed rebellion, he agreed to their demands.

General Nguyen Cao Ky

Here is a biography on Nguyen Cao Ky from what I could find in my research from Wikipedia.

Born Sep. 8, 1930, Vietnam
Died Jul. 23, 2011
Kuala Lumpur, Malaysia

South Vietnamese prime minister and Air Force General Nguyen Cao Ky, was one of South Vietnam's most colorful leaders. In the early 1960s, he rose to the rank of general in the fledgling South Vietnamese Air Force, ultimately becoming its top commander. In 1965, he was chosen as the Prime Minister of the US backed South Vietnamese government by a junta of South Vietnamese generals, despite the fact that he had no political experience. He ruled the country with an iron fist and was able to end the cycle of coups and counter- coups that plagued the country following the assassination of former South Vietnamese Premier Ngo Dinh Diem in 1963. He was also known as a playboy who loved purple scarves, upscale nightclubs and beautiful women. In 1967 he lost the Vietnamese presidential election to his longtime rival, General Nguyen Van Thieu, and then served as Thieu's vice-president from 1967 to 1971. When Saigon fell to the North Vietnamese forces in 1975, he fled the country with his family, ultimately settling in the United States. He was born in 1930 in the Northern Province of Son Tay, west of Hanoi. He grew up under British colonial rule and as a young man became involved in Ho Chi Minh's national liberation movement. He eventually left the movement and later joined the French colonial army, where he trained as a pilot during the French fight against the communist insurgency. After the French defeat in 1954, he fled south to Saigon where he joined the South Vietnamese Air Force. He was married three times, and has six children. He died in a hospital in Kuala Lumpur, Malaysia, where he was being treated for a respiratory ailment.

General Ky would come down to our flight line quite often and just hang out with us. I was in on several conversations he would have with us. He was very interested in our Patricia Lynn RB-57s because he was rated to fly the B-57s.

Our laundry girl that takes care of my barracks is married to a Captain in the V.N.A.F. (Vietnamese Air Force). Capt. Nugun Kene, (not sure of that last name spelling) we call him Capt Ken and he helps his wife pick up clothes quite often. He speaks excellent English as he was trained as a fighter pilot in the U.S. and has become a good friend of Chuck Burton and Myself and would come down on the flight line quite often to visit us. He fly's an A-1H Sky Raider for General Ky and he told us that General Ky was flying the first A-1H that was in the air during the coup. He was probably the one that buzzed the tank that got on the base and parked in front of the F-102s. General Ky stayed up in the air until the squadron could be assembled, that included Capt Ken, then General Ky went back to his office on Tan Son Nhut air base. Capt Ken fly's the only A-1 with a tiger stripe around the tail that we have here on the base. He is famous for his victory rolls when he comes back from an air strike.

Captain Kens A1H Sky Raider

He would come in over the runway at about 300mph and 20 feet off the ground then he goes straight up and rolls around and around then comes in and lands. That was a very exciting month with more to come.

CHAPTER 5

OCTOBER 1964

Mohawk Crash

October 2 1964

Things have now calmed down here after the aborted coup, at least the political problems. Another new guy arrived to help us, Bill Boston from California. Then on Thursday Oct 1st I arrived at work at around 4pm just in time to see an Army OV-1 Mohawk aircraft crash. The Grumman OV-1 Mohawk is an Army armed observation and attack aircraft, designed for battlefield surveillance and light strike capabilities. It is a twin engine, turboprop aircraft and carries two crewmembers with side by side seating.

This Army Mohawk had the right side of his landing gear shot up, and the tire was cocked 90 degrees out of whack. So the fire department foamed the runway right in front of where we were working. This Mohawk is a pretty big aircraft that the Army used for battlefield surveillance and was shot up pretty bad on the right wing and landing gear. They would come in on the runway real fast and hit real hard then bounce back into the air trying to get the wheel straight. On the second try he hit so hard it knocked the wheel and most of the landing gear off. Plus they almost crashed on that second try; he just barely got the aircraft back into the air. They had all kinds of fire trucks out there plus an H43 crash helicopter. We all climbed up on 243s wing to watch what would happen next. There must have been someone important on that aircraft because just then General Moore the Army 2nd Air Division Commander showed up in his staff car. He got out of his car and climbed up on the wing with us to watch. They came in for the last time and hit the runway in the foam and went a few hundred feet and then the main gear broke off and went flying down the runway behind them. Then the aircraft come down on the right wing and tore off the right engine propeller and then the aircraft caught fire. Then the nose gear collapsed and they skidded off the runway into the grass and stopped. Before they even stopped all the fire trucks was pumping foam on the aircraft and the H-43 blew away the flames while the firemen cut open the cockpit and dragged the pilots out, then they put out the rest of the fire. The pilots were ok, they didn't have a scratch on them, and we were all clapping even General Moore and he said that he would make sure those firemen would receive a commendation for their action.

Sunday Oct 4th

We sent 243 into Cambodia to take Pictures along the Ho Chi Minn trail, when they returned to the base we were watching them come in for their landing. They had just touched down on the runway when the left engine literally exploded and fire was trailing out of the back of the engine. Major Musgrove was the pilot and he immediately shut down the engine and the fire went out. They taxied in on one engine and when we inspected the engine we found the remains of a large bird in the engine. Major Musgrove said he saw the bird fly directly into the intake and there was nothing he could do but quickly shut down the engine. This was the first time we ever had to change an engine here in Vietnam and no one had ever done it before except for Chuck Burton and he was in Saigon and we couldn't find him. They change them over at Clark air base when we send them over for their 100hr inspections so this was a first for us. We did have a spare engine on the base just in case so we spent the next 8 hrs figuring out how to change it. We just had everything done and hooked up on the new engine when Chuck showed up so he went over our work and said everything looked good, so let's start it up and see if it runs. Everything looked good and it ran just fine. Major McGinnis took the aircraft up for a test flight and said everything checked good and released the aircraft for combat missions.

Wednesday Oct 14th

We had a scary show at work last night, about 5 or 6 miles from the base. There was a big battle going on and 6 armed A-1H Sky raiders come screaming down the taxiway turned out onto the runway and took off in formation, all 6 of them at once. We could see the Huey helicopters firing with their tracers that looked like a long red line waving up and down and the C-123s were dropping flares. It looked like you were watching a movie. It was quite a show when they would drop their flares and light up the battle field, the Hueys and the A-1Hs would fly in and start shooting tracers and rockets. That battle lasted 2 days and 100 Viet Cong were killed, although that was not an accurate count because the VCs would carry off most of their dead.

The next day the Generals called Major Musgrove to another meeting and informed him they wanted one of our aircraft in the air from 6pm to 6am every night for the next week to see if we could do it with just 2 aircraft. So Sgt Gogdill set up two shifts where the night shift would work from 6pm to 6am and the day shift would work the next night so we would have every other night off. The RF-101s would take all the day targets and we would fly only at night. One aircraft would take off at 6pm and fly for 3hrs then land and the other would take off and fly 3hrs. While one was flying we would refuel, inspect, and fix any problems if there were any. This lasted 5 days then 245 broke down with major radio problems so they decided to end that program until we can get more "Patricia Lynn" aircraft over here.

It has been pretty quiet for the last week or so then on Saturday Oct 24th 245 was taking day pictures in the mountains north of here and got hit with a bullet straight in the right engine intake. It took out most of the compressor blades in the front of the engine. Major Stanfield flew the aircraft back to the base with the engine still running he didn't know what was wrong just that he could only get 60% of the thrust from it. When he taxied in the engine sounded like a steam engine and was vibrating, I could tell that something was wrong with it and when we inspected it we could see immediately that most of the compressor blades were badly damaged. We had used the only spare engine earlier this month on 243 and they had not sent us a new one yet. So that same day they sent us two new engines from Clark AFB on an emergency requisition. This time it only took us

4hrs to change it and flight test the aircraft and then send the aircraft out on a mission. This time we had lots of help even the pilots were helping by doing the refueling and getting the engine ready to install while we were removing the old engine.

Tuesday Oct 27th

The guy who bunked next to me in the barracks was killed. He was a mechanic on one of the C-123 cargo aircraft. He was killed when his C-123 was shot down. They were making an ammunition drop and a Viet Cong bullet hit the ammo in the aircraft and it exploded and they crashed in the jungle and burned. There were eight troops on the aircraft and all were killed. The Pilot was the first U.S. Air Force Academy grad to be killed in the Vietnam War. He had been trying to get me to go with him on a cargo drop and I was planning on going when I had the time. That ended those plans and I was having second thoughts about even riding one of those things down to the beach at Vung Tau but I enjoyed the beach too much.

243sClose Call

Friday night we sent Major Stanfield and Lt Platt on a mission back up in the mountains north of here. When they returned they jumped out of the aircraft almost before we could get the ladder on the side of the cockpit and they were both shaking like a leaf. We asked them what happened and all Major Stanfield could say was he needed a beer. Lt Platt said there were about 50 Viet Cong shooting at them with 50 caliber machine guns as they flew over their target. It was a wonder they didn't get hit the way Lt Platt talked. He said they were firing tracers at them and he could see them coming up all around them. He said one bullet came right up in front of the left wing about 6 inches in front of them. After they flew by the target once the darn fools turned around and went right back through again taking pictures. We checked every inch of the aircraft and they missed them both times. Major Stanfield said there were 2 South Vietnamese A1-H Sky raiders in the area so they called them in and they strafed the area with their guns and then dropped napalm fire bombs on them. They hung around until the A1's were done and took some more pictures and not a single shot was fired at them. Chuck sent Boston over to the operations building and Major Musgrove personally delivered a couple of beers out for Major Stanfield and Lt. Platt. Then sent Boston back to get 3 more beers one for him and for Boston and myself, that was a mistake because Boston come back with a cooler full of beers. Then the 6 of us sat under the wing in the shade and had a couple more beers until they calmed down. Then Sgt Cogdill showed up and wanted to know why we were sitting under the wing drinking beer with the Pilots. We told him what had happened and he said, continue on, he would take care of the aircraft because it was the last flight of the day. He refueled the aircraft and did the post flight inspection than sat down with us and had the last beer. Then Captain Cobb showed up so they sent me (of course) because I was the lowest rank, over to the club for more beer. What a sight, most of the Patricia Lynn crew sitting in the shade on the concrete under the wing of 245 drinking beer and telling war stories. About that time Chuck Nix, my buddy from the RF-101's walked up and said what in the hell are you guys doing, so we told him and offered him a beer. Boston piped up and asked what to do if General Moore should happen to drive by in his staff car? Major Musgrove said; I know General Moore and he would say make room for me and give me a beer. Like I said before, we were a close bunch of guys in a war zone taking care of each other.

CHAPTER 6
NOVEMBER 1964

Bien Hoe Mortar Attack

Sunday Nov 1

A Viet Cong mortar barrage crashed into South Vietnam's second largest air base at 26 minutes past midnight, killing four U S service men, wounding 20 or more others, destroying six B-57 jet bombers and damaging eight others. The B-57s have been stationed at Bien Hoe (Ben WA) airbase northeast of Saigon since the gulf of Tonkin crisis in August.

The 81mm mortar fire was deadly accurate and concentrated on the hanger area and flight line. Besides the six B-57s destroyed and the eight others damaged a helicopter and two A-1s were destroyed, one trying to take off on the runway.

I had only been in bed about an hour when Chuck Burton was shaking me to wake up. He said the base was on alert and we had to get to the aircraft. We woke up Boston and he had just got back from the Airman's club and was pretty drunk, we got him dressed and headed toward the flight line. We were picked up by an Army Jeep that had a loud speaker on it saying "everybody" report to your duty section and draw weapons so they dropped us off at the operations hanger on the flight line. There was a guy in the back handing out brand new AR-15 rifles still in the box, I thought "OH CRAP" what is going on around here. There was a Captain instructing everybody to grab a weapon so I asked him what was going on. He said Bien Hoe airbase was under attack and they figured there were 10,000 Viet Cong surrounding Tan Son Nhut. Anyway I unpacked the AR-15 and assembled it (I was sure glad they checked us out on that weapon at Clark AFB) and then went over where they were handing out ammunition. You should have seen me; I had 3 full magazines (20 in each clip) and 8 boxes of ammo, 20 in each box. I had one clip in the rifle and the rest of my ammo in my pockets. I had a hard time keeping my pants up with 120 rounds on me; they weren't going to catch me shorthanded though. Then as we were leaving they were passing out 45cal pistols with 40 rounds of ammo so I got one of those also. When we arrived at the aircraft I must have looked like a real combat troop with an AR-15 slung over my shoulder and a 45 pistol strapped to my side. When we got to work it was 2:30 in the morning and we sent the rest of the guys from the RF-101s and the F-102s up to the hanger to get their weapons.

We quickly got 243 ready to fly and Major Stanfield and Lt Platt took off and flew up to Bien Hoe to get pictures. We could hear the battle going on up there from Tan Son Nhut because it's only 15 or 20 miles away. But the bad part was we were surrounded ourselves, although the Viet Cong were not attacking us because there must have been 20 armed Huey helicopters patrolling the perimeter of the base. When the aircraft came back, Major Stanfield said all hell was breaking out at Ben Hoe airfield and there were several aircraft destroyed and the Viet Cong were shooting at them when they flew over the base. He thought they had been hit with small arms fire. We inspected the aircraft and found one bullet hole in the horizontal stabilizer. Major Stanfield said not to worry about it because it was not in a critical area and just get the aircraft ready to fly again as soon as possible. Bill Boston and I were the only ones available to take care of the aircraft because the rest of the guys were sent out to guard the RF-101s.

We called a fuel truck out to top off the fuel tanks; Boston was still pretty drunk so I didn't want him up on the wing. I refueled the left-wing and started on the right wing. I adjusted the fuel truck spotlight and was straddling the right tip tank and had just finished filling it when I heard a weird sound go by my head. I looked down at Boston standing next to the truck and asked, what was that? He said he didn't hear anything, just then it happened again and this time I knew what it was. We were being shot at from across the runway about a mile away. The Vietnamese fuel truck driver heard it also and he ran and shut off all the lights on the truck. There were snipers all around the base and obviously they were shooting

David Karmes

at the spotlight on the fuel truck. I jumped down off the wing, ran to the truck, grabbed my AR- 15 rifle and ran for the ditch behind the airplane where they were digging to lay cable. When I looked up there stood Boston with the darndest expression on his face, and said what in the hell are you doing? Just then a Huey helicopter flew right over our heads and started firing at where those shots were coming from with their 20 mm guns. We could see the tracers waving down in the jungle, then about five other helicopters joined in the fight and there was firing going on all over the place over there. Then Boston ran to the truck grabbed his AR- 15 ran back and jumped in the ditch with me and now he was stone cold sober, he finally figured out what was happening. He said I jumped off the wing ran to the truck grabbed my rifle and was in that ditch in about 2 seconds, and he couldn't figure out what I was doing; now he knew. I would've been all right though if I hadn't been so stupid. I turned the spotlight on the fuel truck on the tip tank so I could see what I was doing instead of using a flashlight. There I was sitting in that bright light. You can bet that I will never do that again.

 I saw the pictures they took of Bien Hoe airfield; they flat tore up the base with mortar fire. We went to an intelligence briefing with the pilots Sunday morning and they showed us the pictures that 243 took. Gen. William C Westmoreland, commander of US forces in South Vietnam also attended that meeting. You could just glance at the pictures and see where they concentrated their fire. Right on the 20 B-57s that were parked on the ramp. Four of them got direct hits and burned right to the ground, some of them had wings blown off, tails blown off, and nose sections blown off. Plus some caught on fire from the others burning. Then some only got hit by flying debris. It looks like I might end up there helping repair the ones that had minor damage. I don't know yet but I will know by the end of the week. Six of them were completely destroyed and eight of them were damaged.

 They patched up the rest of them and flew all of them to Clark Air Force Base in the Philippines for major repair, so I didn't need to go. I was happy to hear that I didn't have to go because it was very dangerous up there. The American casualty toll from the Bien Hoe airbase attack Sunday was revised upward to 76 Tuesday with the release of later figures by the U.S. command in South Vietnam, the original, was 36. The additional casualties were among servicemen who received minor wounds, unreported because the men went back on duty or to their Barrack's after receiving first aid. Four men were killed in the Viet Cong mortar bombardment one was in critical condition, two were listed as seriously injured and 15 others remain hospitalized. Although twice as large as the original 36, the new casualty total was actually less severe, since it contained fewer seriously injured or hospitalized personnel. US military headquarters in Saigon meanwhile ruled out any negligence on the part of U.S. Air Force commanders in the crippling of America's jet bomber fleet in the Communist raid on Sunday. Thousands of rockets and bombs were unleashed against the positions from which Communist guerrillas were suspected of shelling the base but had no effect. The closest bomb crater was more than 50 yards from the area where government troops discovered the imprints of mortar base plates. General Westmoreland, Ambassador, Maxwell D Taylor, Premier Major general Nguyen Khanh, and Major General Nguyen Ky flew up to the base and set up a formal investigation to fix responsibility for the security failure that accounted for the guerrilla success at Bien Hoe airbase November 8, 1964

US combat planes throughout Vietnam were ordered to disburse on all the bases. Now we have our airplanes scattered all over the base so if they start throwing mortars in here they won't get all of them. Our two aircraft were left where they are but the rest of the combat Jets were moved to different spaces all over the base, some of them so far that we had to have helicopters take the crews to them when they wanted to fly. This only lasted a week because it was such a hassle for the air crews and the ground crews. When the mechanics would call for a fuel truck it would sometime take the driver an hour just to find out where the aircraft was located. Also if they had to scramble the F-102 interceptors they couldn't get them all together at one time and they would have a terrible time trying to get them in the air.

Later that week some Viet Cong were trying to break into the ammo dump, it's just down the way from where we are located. They dropped flares over it so they could see and there was a lot of gunfire going on around the ammo dump. The guards killed four of them before they could even get near the ammo dump. Then one of the flares drifted over the flight line, I was just putting the canopy down on my aircraft when I saw it

David Karmes

coming, it was headed right for an RF- 101 so I ran over to the aircraft and climbed up on the RF- 101 with a broom handle I got out of the truck. It was still smoldering so I couldn't let it land on the airplane or it might set it afire. The darn thing drifted out of my reach and headed toward another aircraft. So I jumped down and got up on the other one just before it hit. I hooked it with a broom handle and let it down to the ground.

The next day things calmed down and they cleared all the Viet Cong from around the base. Our security here is much better than they had at Bien Hoe so we don't seem to have any problem at this time with the Viet Cong. We had to turn in our AR-15s, even though I did not want to, but we kept our 45 cal pistols. I kind of liked pretending to be a combat troop. But I know now where I can get them in a hurry.

Saturday, Nov. 14, 1964

I was helping my friend Chuck Nix with his RF- 101; he needed to change a tire before we could head out for town. They had his aircraft parked in an area where an aircraft had just come in with a load of dead South Vietnamese troops. There were a bunch of family members waiting on the flight line not knowing if their husband or son was on that plane. That is one kind of hell I hope we never have to go through. There was a pretty little Vietnamese girl that had just lost her husband, walk away from the airplane crying and carrying two little kids. After I saw that I never went down there again and Chuck had his aircraft moved back to the flight line where it was before they moved all the aircraft. I can't really condemn the Air Force for sending me over here because somebody had to come. If I had to be away from my wife for a year it's not such a bad price to pay if it will help these people win this war so they can live like we do. I can still picture that little girl with her two kids to this very day over 50 years ago; so sad.

I get to fly in my aircraft

Monday, Nov.16, 1964

Sgt. Cogdill, came over to the barracks and woke me up and told me to pack my bag because I was going to Clark Air Force Base in the Philippines with my airplane. There is a typhoon heading this way and they are evacuating all the aircraft, you should see this place it's a madhouse. We have to get everything off the flight line that would blow away because they are expecting over 100 miles-per-hour winds. There are 20 aircraft at a time lined up on the taxi way waiting to take off. I had to go to base operations and get fitted for a helmet and I will fly in the backseat of 245 with Major Stanfield and one of the new guys will fly in 243 with Major McGinnis. We were not in any big hurry to take off because we had top priority and could go ahead of all of the other aircraft that are waiting to take off. We sat around for a while and watched some of the aircraft take off. Then we started the engines, and taxied out ahead of all of the other aircraft and took off. We hooked up with 243 and were flying in formation which was really neat; we had just passed over the coast of South Vietnam and were headed out over the South China Sea toward the Philippines when they called us back. The typhoon had changed course and wasn't going to hit the base after all, so we come back and landed. The four of us were really disappointed and we wish we had taken off earlier because then they could not have called us back because we would not have had enough fuel. Plus the Majors were going to buy us dinner at the real plush officers club on the base at Clark AFB. I sure could have used some real milk at Clark and a two or three day vacation from this place. Here in Vietnam we can't get real milk, only canned milk and it's something that everyone here missed. Although every now and then we would beg some off from the stewardess's that come in on the Pan-American 707's. We didn't get hit by that typhoon, but I got to fly in my B- 57 even though it was for only about 40 min.

Bombed in Saigon

November 28, 1964

It looks like things are starting to get hot around here again; a bomb went off here on the base at the Tan Son Nhut civilian air terminal this morning and hurt a lot of people. Then that afternoon the Viet Cong bombed the Navy dispensary downtown and killed four people. To top it all off, two of the RF- 101 guys and I went to town that night and we were in a bar on Tuo Do Street sitting at the bar drinking beer when a bomb went off across the street at another bar. The explosion was so large it knocked us off our seats. A witness said that a motorbike rolled by and threw a bomb and it hit the screen in the front. It blew out the whole front of the bar but nobody was hurt. We decided to go back to Tan Son Nhut and finish our night at the airman's club where it was safe. It will probably get a lot hotter here in the next few months. The students are demonstrating again causing a lot of problems in town. The next day they restricted us to the base again until things calm down.

CHAPTER 7

DECEMBER 1964

F100 Crash

December 4, 1964

An F- 100 on his way to Da Nang up north stopped here at Saigon for fuel. I was on the wing of my airplane and I watched him taxi out toward the other end of the runway and get ready to take off. He started his takeoff roll and hit the engine afterburner and started down the runway, the aircraft left the ground and was about three quarters down the runway and just as he got airborne I heard a loud explosion and his engine quit. His landing gear was still down so he set it down on the runway and popped his drag chute, but he didn't have room to stop before the end of the runway.

    He hit the brakes and literally burned both tires right off then he skidded off the runway and sent up a big cloud of dust, the nose gear collapsed and he skidded across the taxiway and run the nose of the aircraft right into the ground. When he stopped he was only about 50 yards from where I was. He opened his canopy and he just sat there looking dazed. I jumped off the wing of my aircraft and run out there to help him. When I got to the airplane he just sat there and looked at me. Both of his main landing gear tires were on fire and fuel was spilling out of the aircraft. I hollered at him to put the safety pins in your ejection seat and get out, the aircraft is on fire. He located the safety pins for his ejection seat and installed them and then I helped him get his parachute off and helped him out of the aircraft. When he hit the ground we run like hell because the aircraft was on fire. We had just cleared the area when the fire department arrived and foamed down the whole airplane so it didn't burn up or explode. That airplane will never fly again, because it was completely destroyed. The pilot didn't get hurt except he was shaking pretty bad. He wasn't the only one that was shaking and he gave me a big hug and said he owed me one. When Sgt. Ware came out of the trailer to see what had happened he told me to go ahead and take the rest of the day off, so I went over to the Airman's club and had a couple of drinks to calm down.

December 14, 1964

We were waiting for 243 to return from a mission and all the fire trucks went out to the runway and sure enough they were out there for our aircraft. They were coming in on emergency and they came down and landed normally and everything seemed to be okay, they taxied in and stopped. Maj. Stanfield was the pilot so when I put the ladder up and crawled up the ladder I asked him what the problem was. He said look over at the right wing, I looked over there and there was a hole in the wing about the size of a basketball.

They had been flying the canals down in the Mekong Delta when they were hit by what appeared to be a 20 mm cannon. It hit the bottom of the wing and come right through to the top; it was a straight shot clean through the wing so it didn't do any damage inside. There was an access panel right next to where the bullet went in. We removed the panel and we could see that there was no damage to any of the spars or any other internal part of the wing. Just then Chuck Burton drove up in the metro van and I hollered at him to come see what Major Stanfield did to his aircraft. Then Major Stanfield spoke up and said you should've seen the ones that I had to fly around that missed us. We called out the sheet metal guys and they patched up the wing and we put the aircraft back into service. Maj. Stanfield confided in us later that it seems they were getting shot at more and more. That's why they like to fly at night; they don't have to worry about being shot at

New Aircraft (237) Arrives

December 20, 1964

I arrived at work approximately an hour early and went in the trailer. I told the guys that I saw one of our aircraft was in the pattern and landing, they looked at me like I was crazy and they said that both of our aircraft are parked out on the ramp, what was I talking about? I opened the door and looked out on the ramp and sure enough there were both our aircraft parked out there and another Patricia Lynn aircraft was taxiing down the taxiway. Everybody jumped up and went out on the parking ramp just as the aircraft was turning in to our parking area. One of our new aircraft had just arrived, serial number 55-4237. We found a spot to park the aircraft and helped the pilots get out. They had just come in from Clark Air Force Base where they had taken the ferry tank out of the Bombay and put in all the new upgraded camera equipment. For some reason they had neglected to tell us that they were on their way, otherwise we might have been ready for them. The pilot reported there were no problems with the aircraft so we refueled and inspected it real close and found that this airplane was in beautiful shape, it looked like it just came off the assembly line. There was some new upgraded camera equipment installed and the infrared system had been upgraded. It also had the new ground clearance radar installed in a pod under the right wing. Now we have three aircraft that we have to take care of, plus now we have another flight crew. They also told us there is another aircraft over at Clark Air Force Base getting the new camera equipment installed in it and should be here in a few days.

Bob Hope Sneaks into Vietnam

December 24, 1964

We were just coming back from the chow hall around 4pm when we noticed a bunch of staff cars were lined up over at the Air Vietnam terminal, then this C-54 passenger aircraft taxied in and stopped next to them. We stopped to see what was going on, we thought maybe it was a five-star General because of all of the staff cars, but when the people got out, it wasn't a five-star General it was a SIX star General{Bob Hope}and his troupe. We knew he was in Korea entertaining the troops there, but we didn't think that he would be allowed to come into a combat zone. Hope's troupe included Anita Bryant, Jill St, John, Janis Paige, Miss World, 20 year old Anne Sidney, Anna Maria Alberghetti, Jerry Colonna, Peter Leeds, John Bubbles, and Less Brown and his band. Hope's arrival in Vietnam was not announced in advance and no one on the base knew when he was coming, except for us because we caught him when he landed. It was not announced in advance because officials said that large crowds of Americans turning out in Vietnam to see Hope would form ideal targets for Viet Cong communist attacks. Bob Hope was now in a live combat zone as he would soon find this out. There is no behind the lines in Vietnam and he and his fellow entertainers will face the same dangers from communist Viet Cong terrorist as the 22,000 American servicemen they are here to entertain.

The former commander-in-chief of American forces here, Gen. Paul D Harkins felt so strongly about this that he turned down the famous comedians bids to perform for his troops at Christmas last year and in 1962. General Harkins big worry was that huge crowds of American servicemen turning out to see Hope would give a tempting and vulnerable target to communist killer squads. This year in 1964, Hope convinced our new American commander Gen. William C Westmoreland, to let him come and entertain the troops. Gen. Westmoreland is an outspoken believer in the importance of his soldier's morale and he eagerly accepted Hopes request.

They loaded the group into the staff cars and their baggage onto a flatbed truck and started into Saigon to the fashionable Caravelle Hotel, where they would be staying and would operate out of that hotel as he entertained the troops throughout South Vietnam. As Hope and his group were driving into Saigon from the airport a huge blast occurred when they were only a few blocks from their hotel. The Viet Cong had planted a bomb in the main US officers billet in downtown Saigon, the Brinks Hotel.

The Brinks Hotel is where all of our pilots lived in downtown Saigon and where we would occasionally spend the night on one of their couches if we could not get back to the base before midnight curfew. About 123 US officers lived in the building and at 6 PM when the explosion took place, many were in their quarters. Luckily none of our pilots were injured. When the blast occurred security agents sent Hope's baggage truck racing back to the airport but he convinced them to let him and his group continue on to their hotel. When he arrived the Brinks Hotel was still in flames and there was extensive damage to many of the neighboring buildings, including the Continental Hotel which was located alongside the Brinks. Windows were broken at the Caravelle hotel which is across the street from the Brink's about 100 yards away from where his 60 member group would be staying. The blast came as many of Saigon's Roman Catholics were finishing their Christmas shopping and nearby streets were thrown into panic. There were estimates that the bomb set off at the hotel may have been as big as a 500 pounder. Someone planted it on or near the ground floor perhaps in the generator room, perhaps in a parked car.

It demolished the Armed Forces radio station operating on the ground floor next to the generator room. This station provided entertainment, news and general information throughout South Vietnam. The movie Good Morning Vietnam was about that radio station. One of our officers Maj. Pruitt was just driving up to the compound gate in his car; he told us when the thing went off, there was a blast and a fireball and things were flying everywhere. The blast destroyed the first three floors of the 7 story building and it had to be evacuated. Two Americans were killed, one officer and one civilian. Two other American civilians were wounded that lived in the quarters. The wounded included 29 Army, 11 Air Force, 13 Navy and 2 Marine officers.

After Hope and his troupe were settled in at the hotel he and some of his people went to the Navy hospital where the injured had been taken. They said in the base paper they gave blood and Hope personally shook the hand of 42 of the injured before he left to go to dinner. At dinner he dined with American ambassador Maxwell D Taylor and the Commander of US forces in Saigon, Gen. William C Westmoreland. At dinner ambassador Taylor noted that Hope had blood on the cuffs of his shirt after personally shaking hands with the 42 American victims. Hope said, I didn't realize I had the bloodstains, he was surprised. What a great man he was.

December 25, 1964

Christmas day, Bob Hope showed up at Tan Son Nhut early that morning and Hope and some of his troupe boarded his aircraft. They flew down to Vinh Long, an American helicopter base in the heart of Viet Cong Territory. The base paper said Hope and his troupe performed in Vinh Long 70 miles southeast of Saigon on the back of a flatbed truck for about 400 helicopter pilots and maintenance men. Sandbag bunkers were lined up behind the truck on which Hope, Jill St. John, Jerry Colonna, Janis Paige and Anna Marie Alberghetti performed. The boom of artillery firing at suspected Vietcong positions was heard in the background. All of the men in the audience were armed but there was no sign of Viet Cong activity.

Hope and his company flew back to Saigon Christmas day for an afternoon show before 3000 servicemen at Tan Son Nhut airport which I attended. He came out on the stage with a golf club in one hand and a beautiful girl, (Miss World) Ann Sidney, in the other. You could tell he was jumpy and his whole cast was the same way. During the show you could hear the 105 Howitzer's firing off about 10 miles in the distance. South Vietnam A1-H fighters and U.S. Huey armed helicopters patrolled the perimeter. We also sent up 3 F-102 interceptors to patrol the area.

Hope commented, well we came over here where the action is and we got a little more than expected, but that's okay. He joked, a funny thing happened to me when I was driving through downtown Saigon to my hotel last night; we met a hotel going the other way. He made a few more jokes about it, like I've never seen a house detective in full flight before and I was sent over here to give you live entertainment, so let's keep it that way. It was a great show and we all really enjoyed it and anyone who has ever seen him perform before the troops will never forget it.

He was a great man and the U.S. commander in Vietnam Gen. William C Westmoreland presented Hope with a commemorative plaque. The show from Tan Son Nhut was shown on TV in the U.S. on January 15, 1965. Just as the show got started and they were filming for TV my aircraft flew over real low taking pictures and banked right over the stage, the TV cameras turned on it because Bob Hope said to get a good shot of it. I tried to get some of the pictures the aircraft took but was never able to. The next day he and his troupe were off to Bien Hoa to entertain the troops there.

Dec 30, 1964

Bill Boston and I had planned on going to the movie tonight, because there were no flights scheduled. Sgt Cogdill hunted us down at the Airman's club, because we were the only guys he could find. There is a really hot target they need to get tonight and they are flying all 3 aircraft twice. The 3 of us had six 2 hr. flights to take care of. The last one came down at 5 AM and we finished up at 7 AM. Between the three aircraft they flew the Ho Chi Mhin trail for 12 total hours before they got the target they needed. All three aircrews were totally exhausted and the three of us were also exhausted. All three of the aircraft came back with no damage and no mechanical problems, what a great testament to the B-57 aircraft.

Dec 31, 1964

Our 90 day temporary duty guys from Japan are leaving today so all three of them have cleared the base and Chuck Burton is on CQ duty for a week over at the tent city. Hutch is in the hospital with gallbladder trouble; Tech Sgt. Smith is working today with Sgt. Cogdill. So that leaves me for the night shift. Tonight I will be the only one there to take care of both flights so I'm going to get a workout again tonight. At least Smitty and Sgt. Cogdill will have them all ready for me when I get there. When I arrived at work Smitty hung around and helped me get both aircraft off on their missions. When both aircraft returned around 10 pm from their missions there were no mechanical problems. Because it was New Years Eve the pilots felt sorry for me so they helped me. They did the refueling while I did the post flight inspections and closed up the aircraft for the night. Then I took both of the air crews to the Airman's club with me where a special band from the Philippines was playing and we rang in the New Year. Like I said before we have the best club on the base, not to mention the best pilots.

CHAPTER 8

JANUARY 1965

January 3, 1965

We have all three of our aircraft on night combat missions and all three of our aircraft came back broken. We worked 12 straight hours to get them back in flying condition. Aircraft 243 needed a new starter on the left hand engine, 245 had a bad generator on the right-hand engine and 237 was having rudder problems. We repaired all three of them and have been flying all three of them every night for the last four days with no problems.

Monday, January 7, 1965

Aircraft 55-4249 that was at Clark Air Force Base getting the fuel ferry tank removed and the new camera equipment installed arrived today. The pilot said he was having problems with the left engine. We checked it out and had to replace the fuel control. It took four days to get parts from Clark Air Force Base and change it. Major Stanfield flew it and tested everything, then released it for combat missions. I was assigned as the crew chief on that new aircraft. Meanwhile Chuck Burton and I have been flying the other three aircraft every night this week while the day shift fixed 249 and fixed some minor problems with the other three aircraft.

My new Aircraft

My new aircraft

New Weird Bomb

Wednesday, January 9, 1965

I just arrived at work and in the flight pattern over the base were Six F-100 fighter-bombers. They landed and taxied into the jet parking area. Now we have six F-100 Super Saber fighter bombers, six F-102 Delta Dagger interceptors, twelve RF-101 Voo Doo reconnaissance Jets and four RB-57 infrared equipped reconnaissance Jets in our crowded jet parking area. We had been expecting the F-100s because their maintenance people were already here and they had prepared a parking place for them. They will remain on the base for now and they said they possibly may move to Da Nang air base up north in the near future. We talked with the mechanics that were with the aircraft and they said that they had been over at Clark Air Force Base in the Philippines practicing with a new bomb that they had brought with them. It seems they have this bomb that was filled with little ball bearings and that when they release it; it spreads out over the jungle and will kill anything under it. There is no explosive in it, it just opens up and spreads out over a wide area and goes real fast to the ground.

The next day they had occasion to use the new bomb, there was a firefight about 20 miles North of the base in the jungle so they sent three of the F 100's loaded with the bombs up to see how they would work. I had just arrived at work and was watching them take off with their mechanics. Each aircraft had two bombs one under each wing. This was their first combat mission and the guys were excited that their aircraft were on their first mission. It did not go well. According to one of their pilots. He said everything was going fine except they had to be extremely careful, because the ball bearings spread over such a large area and they didn't want to hit any of our allied troops. But that was only a minor problem compared to what happened next. The pilot that had the last bomb decided that he would go to a higher altitude to drop this one. Then one of the other F-100s not realizing what he did, flew directly into the ball bearings after the bomb had opened, what a mess.

It was about an hour and a half after we had watched them take off that I noticed that the fire trucks were going out onto the runway. Everybody stopped to see what was coming in on emergency, then one of the F-100 crew Chiefs came over and said that one of their airplanes had been hit and was in pretty bad shape. We could see him off in the distance coming straight in on emergency and the whole airplane seemed to be smoking like maybe it was on fire. There was another F-100 flying directly beside him and as they came to the far end of the runway he touched down onto the runway and the smoke that was coming out of the back of the airplane was coming from the jet engine. The pilot was not out of the woods yet though, there were all kinds of fluids leaking from the aircraft. Jet fuel, hydraulic fluid and even liquid oxygen was pumping out of the side of the airplane. He didn't have any brakes because all of the hydraulic fluid had leaked out. When he reached our end of the runway he was still going pretty fast but he did manage to turn off on the last exit to the taxiway and coasted into our parking area. Like I said what a mess. The aircraft was full of holes about the size of marbles, they were everywhere in the wings, in the fuselage, in the tail, and even the canopy was broken. It so damaged the engine it was a wonder that he made it back to the base, but it was still running when he touched down on the runway. It literally totaled the aircraft, it never flew again and they robbed what parts they could get out of it and pushed it off in the corner. Now we only have five F-100 fighter bombers. But their problems were not over, a few days later they had a new mission.

A few days earlier Major Stanfield and Lt Platt were taking pictures in 237 over the communist held plain of Jars in Laos. The pictures showed a large buildup of communist troops and materials along route seven, a key road and part of the Ho Chi Minh trail in Laos over which supplies and men reach communist guerrillas in South Vietnam and central Laos. The road extends northwestward from North Vietnam toward the Communist held plain of Jars in Laos. Connecting with this road are other roads leading into the Laotian Panhandle and then by trail into South Vietnam. This seemed like a great time to use the new bomb the F-100's had. So they sent all five of them to attack them along that road. They did a lot of damage to all of the supplies and the troops that were there, but one of the F-100s was shot down and the pilot was killed. Now we have only four F-100 fighter-bombers. But it wasn't over yet, a few days later one of the F-100's blew a tire on takeoff skidded off the runway and run head long into a pile of rocks that they had piled up for the new runway. The pilot was not hurt but the aircraft was totaled so they pushed it off to the side with the other one. A few days later they transferred the remaining three F-100's to Da Nang airbase up North.

Then a few days later we were waiting for 243 to return from a mission when a C-123 with 16 Americans aboard crashed into that same pile of rocks. The two-engine C-123 apparently had a runaway propeller that pulled it to one side on takeoff. The aircraft blew a tire and skidded into the large rock pile near the runway breaking up as it hit.

All 16 persons aboard were Americans bound for the coastal town of Nha Trang two hundred miles northeast of here. The flight was described as a routine logistics flight, although the guys were headed to the coast for a little R&R. We heard the crash when it hit, when we looked up all we could see was smoke and dust. When the dust cleared we could see the troops running out from behind the aircraft, they had run down the open rear ramp. But the aircraft was on fire and the pilot was coming out of the front window, when he jumped he broke his ankle, he was the only one hurt.

First Combat Mission for My new Aircraft

January 16, 1965

Major Musgrove and Captain Cobb flew 249s first combat mission and it was a disaster. When they returned they were coming in on emergency. All the fire trucks went out to the runway. Base operations called me on the radio in the truck and said they had been hit and Major Musgrove was injured. Then an ambulance arrived in the parking area. The landing looked good and when they taxied in we could see a big hole in the right side of the cockpit and the canopy was broken. They were going real slow down the taxiway because they had no brakes because of loss of hydraulic fluid. Then they turned into the parking ramp and Major Musgrove shut down the engines and coasted to a stop in the middle of the parking ramp. I put the ladder up on the aircraft and the medics scrambled up the ladder to help Major Musgrove. He just sat there looking dazed and I could tell he was about to pass out. I hollered at the medics to stop and I went up the ladder and sure enough Major Musgrove had not put the safety seat pins in the ejection seat and if they would've tried to lift him out, they might have set off that ejection seat. I put the safety pins in the seat and the three of us helped the Major, who was coming in and out of consciousness, to get out onto the ladder and down and into the ambulance where they immediately started an IV in his arm. They, then, took off for the hospital.

Captain Cobb said they were flying low in the mountains up north and their target was in a valley. They were flying between two mountains and had been hit with a 50 caliber bullet. The bullet had come in the right side of the forward cockpit and hit a hydraulic line and bounded around the canopy and cut two groves in it and cracked it in several places and hit major Musgrove in the right arm. It also hit the instrument panel and damaged a lot of instruments. There was blood and hydraulic fluid all over the cockpit, it was a real mess. Captain Cobb said Major Musgrove flew the aircraft for 10 minutes trying to bandage up the hole in his arm. He ordered Capt. Cobb that if he passed out from lack of blood that he was to eject out of the aircraft. The pilot has the only controls to fly the aircraft. He did manage to stop the bleeding using the first aid kit that he had in his flight suit, although he lost a lot of blood. Captain Cobb said it was really touch and go the last 5 min. of flying. While they were in the pattern to land he was coming in and out of consciousness from lack of blood. Captain Cobb said he was thanking God when they hit that runway because he knew they were going to make it even if they ran off the end of the runway because of lack of brakes. Major Musgrove was not hurt bad, it was only a flesh wound and they kept him in the hospital for two days and he was back flying the next week. What an awesome commander and pilot this man was.

Wow, did it ever tear up the inside of the cockpit, it took us a week to clean up the blood and hydraulic fluid in the cockpit, repair the hydraulic lines, fix the hole in the side of the cockpit, replace most of the instruments and the canopy. When we got everything repaired, Major Stanfield flew it on a test flight and everything checked out okay and he released it for combat missions. It was a brand-new aircraft and here it gets all shot up on its first combat mission.

When major Musgrove returned to work on Monday we all went over to his office to see how he was. He said he flew P- 38 fighters in World War II and F-86 jet fighters in the Korean War. He was an ace in World War II shooting down five aircraft with his P-38 and two Migs with his F-86 in the Korean War. He said his aircraft had been shot up several times in those two wars and he had to bailout twice, once in the P-38 and he had to eject once out of his F- 86 jet fighter. But he himself had never been hurt until he comes to Vietnam and some guy standing on the ground gets him. Major Musgrove said they were flying low between two mountains when the 50 caliber hit them. Captain Cobb said he was quite concerned when the Major told him he may have to eject if he passed out from lack of blood and from now on the Captain said let's not fly between the mountains anymore. Although they did many times more because that was the only way they could get low enough to get their target. What a great man our commander was, I tried to find out more about him while writing this book but failed.

January 23, 1965

My new aircraft that I am now the crew chief on 55-4249 is back ready for combat missions after Major Stanfield test flew it and released it. Major Musgrove and Captain Cobb will fly it again on its second combat mission. Here we go again, when they came back all the fire trucks went out to the runway and sure enough 249 was in trouble again and this time they were hit in the tail with another 50 caliber and were having trouble with the rudder, plus when they lowered the landing gear they had a down and locked left landing gear light flickering on and off. They flew low right down the flight line and over the tower so the guys in the tower could check the underside of the aircraft and the landing gear for damage before they landed. You could see the hole just behind the bomb bay in the tail and the landing gear looked okay. The bullet went in underneath and it messed up the control linkage to the rudder. The landing gear was okay, when we checked it we found the light in the cockpit was defective. Major Musgrove, with his arm still bandaged up, landed the aircraft with no trouble. When he taxied in and stopped, I put up the ladder and climbed up and looked him straight in the eye and told him I didn't want him to fly my aircraft anymore. The next time you want to go flying take one of the other aircraft. He laughed and said he agreed with me, although he flew it many more times with only minor problems. Although it was hit several times more, with only minor damage. There was only minor damage to the rudder linkage, we repaired it and repaired the hole in the fuselage and Major Stanfield had to test fly it again and released it again for combat flight.

Sand bag Revetments

You should see our Jet parking area now; you would think this was a war zone or something. We have sandbag revetments for our aircraft piled up 8 foot high, 6 foot wide and 40 feet long. They have 20 of them built now and they are building more. We will park our airplanes between them. It really looks weird, there is going to be enough for all of the F-102's, the F-101's and our RB- 57's. They are mortar bunkers for the airplanes so if a mortar hits one aircraft it won't burn down the one parked next to it. I pity those poor guys that are building them. There are 5,000 sandbags in each sandbag revetment and they have to fill them by hand and each sandbag weighs about 70lbs each. Since the attack on Bien Hoa last fall that destroyed so many of our B-57's up there, they decided we needed to protect our aircraft from Mortar attack here at Tan Son Nhut airfield. They turned out to be quite handy, because when we were off duty we would get a six pack of beer and sit on top of them and watch the aircraft take off and land and occasionally crash.

Sandbags

Also a blast fence was installed between our parking area and the taxiway.

That worked out real good because when we run the engines or when the pilots were ready to taxi and there was an aircraft coming down the taxiway, we were so close to the taxiway we would have to cut the engines back to idle.

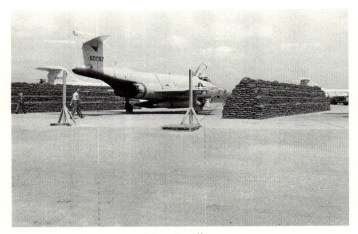

More Sandbags

January 28, 1965.

Chuck Burton and I are off today so we decided to go to the swimming pool in Saigon. We had just changed our clothes and were relaxing in our chairs before getting ready to get in the water. All of a sudden the U.S. Army MP's (Military Police) stormed into the area and ordered everyone out of the pool and to leave the area. They told us to grab our clothes and leave the area before we could even change into them. It seems they found 40 pounds of explosives next to the fence. If that had exploded it probably would have killed every one in the pool and it was set to go off that afternoon. That was really a close one; our chairs were only about 20 feet from the fence where they found the explosives. So we grabbed a cab and headed back to Tan Son Nhut where it is somewhat safe.

CHAPTER 9

FEBUARY 1965

Burn Down the Black Forest

Feb 3 1965

We have been having a series of targets in an area in the Black Forest for the last few days. The Black Forest is located north of Saigon up near the central highland city of Da Lat; it is thick impenetrable jungle type of forest. The pictures were showing a large buildup of Viet Cong and possibly North Vietnamese troops plus a large amount of equipment.

One of the guys I hang out with lives in the same barracks that I do, he is a crew chief on one of the C-1 23 cargo planes we have here. We were at the airman's club having a few drinks; he was telling us about a big operation that was soon to take place. Due to the Viet Cong buildup in the Black Forest, the people running this war decided we needed to burn part of the forest down. They have been gathering C-123 cargo aircraft from all over Southeast Asia plus the Philippines, Japan and even Australia. They are gathering anything that will burn and putting it in 55 gallon drums, things like old hydraulic fluid, engine drain oil, and mostly aircraft and jet fuel. Whenever an aircraft or helicopter is defueled they cannot reuse it so they store it in 55 gallon drums, and every now and then the fire department will use it for practice. They planned on having 50 aircraft, each with 50- fifty-five gallon drums aboard. The plan was to drop them into the jungle with an explosive that would go off when they hit the ground.

My friend was best friends with my bunkmate John that lived next to me and John was killed in September. He knew that I had planned to go with John when they did an ammunition delivery so he asked me if I would go with him and help him on this operation. He assured me that they will be flying high enough to avoid any ground fire. All we had to do was push the drums out the back of the aircraft when the pilot said to. I had already been shot at and didn't care to be shot at again. He said it would be an interesting and safe mission and I agreed. I told him I would have to check with Sgt Cogdill and if he Ok'ed it I would go. Sgt Cogdill said to go ahead and go with them when they go, he didn't care because we have been getting more help for the last two months. He said it might be interesting and would like to go also, but he can't, but let him know how it went.

The day before the big mission my aircraft come back from a mission with left engine problems. We were going to need to replace the fuel control plus one of the generators. So I didn't get to go, I had to get my aircraft back in flying condition.

When the day came for the operation, C-123 aircraft were coming in to Tan Son Nhut airfield from all over the area. When they were assembled we had 30 C-123s take off from Tan Son Nhut loaded with 50 fifty-five gallon drums each, plus they hooked up with 20 more C-123s from other bases for a total of 50 aircraft.

When Bill returned, he told us over some beers at the airman's club what had happened. They flew in waves, 10 aircraft at a time over the area they wanted to burn. He was in the first wave and they flew wingtip to wingtip. They pushed all 50 drums out of all 10 aircraft at the same time, then they went up to a higher altitude and circled the area and watched as the other aircraft dropped their loads. When the drums hit the ground most of them did not explode. So they called in several A-1H Sky Rader fighter-bombers with napalm bombs. The A-1H would come in low over the jungle and then drop their napalm bombs. They set off most of the 55 gallon drums and there was a huge firestorm. They managed to burn down most of the area they were after. Bill told us that compared to the amount of effort that was put into the operation; he didn't think they accomplished much. Later they found out the Viet Cong just went underground and escaped the fire. Although they did destroy a lot of the Viet Cong's equipment that was above ground. He did say I missed out on a great adventure, and it was fun pushing those 50 gallon drums out of the back of the aircraft, although it turned out to be more dangerous than he said it would be. On one of the aircraft the drum exploded just as it was going out the back of the aircraft. If it would have been inside five more feet they would've lost the whole aircraft.

Two days later my friend was wounded. Here is the report from the base paper. Two Americans were wounded by shell fragments Tuesday when an Air Force C-1 23 transport plane was hit by Viet Cong fire. The two engine transport was hit over Binh Duong province 20 miles North of Saigon. Neither American was seriously injured. The Viet Cong had announced that they would not fire on unarmed Vietnamese soldiers during the lunar New Year holiday. Presumably the cease-fire did not include Americans. No significant military activity was reported anywhere else in the country. My friend now has a purple heart to take home with him

February 5, 1965

We just found out we lost one of our friends last month. We would occasionally drink with him and some of our pilots over in Cholon at the Army hotel. I didn't know him very well but he was good friends with some of our pilots. Although I think everybody in Vietnam knew of him he was a Med-Evac helicopter pilot.

His name was Charles E. Kelly and I think everybody in Vietnam talks about him.

Major Kelly was commanding officer of those choppers, "the 57th medical detachment," the "helicopter ambulances and there wasn't anyplace he wouldn't take them to get a wounded man out. He was killed on one of those missions. From what some of the guys say he was quite a man and will be missed greatly. He will be remembered for a long time. These guys that fly these helicopters were amazing.

C-47 Cargo Aircraft Crash

February 7 1965

A lot of times I will go to work early and sit around and watch the aircraft take off and land "just for something to do". Also we have a horse shoe range set up behind the aircraft and there's always someone playing horse shoes. A lot of the guys from the RF- 101s and the F- 102s do the same thing I do, so there is always someone around to play with before work and during work while the aircraft are flying. There were four of us playing and it was a real nice day, although it was hot as always, but there was a nice wind coming across the runway so the aircraft were having to land and take off in a cross wind which is interesting to see.

All of a sudden we hear a loud popping noise and coming down the runway, on takeoff was a South Vietnamese C- 47 cargo aircraft loaded with paratroopers. The left engine was backfiring, "that is what we were hearing". The aircraft was airborne about 200 feet above the runway when the left engine quit. The South Vietnamese pilot did the exact thing that you do not want to do, he turned into the dead engine or maybe the cross wind pushed him that way. Then we could see the aircraft shaking just before it stalled out and crashed on the second runway that was under construction.

We could see some of the crew that was working on the new runway running for their lives when they saw that C-47 coming at them. There was a huge cloud of dust and we could not see the aircraft anymore, then out of that dust cloud came running about 30 South Vietnamese paratroopers. By this time the control tower had seen what happened and had the fire trucks on their way to the aircraft. They had to stop short of the aircraft because of the dust cloud that the troops were still appearing from, when the dust settled everybody got out of the aircraft and there was no one injured, although the C- 47 was completely destroyed. There must have been fuel leaking out of the aircraft because it exploded in a ball fire at least five or 10 min. after the crash. It was amazing that none of the crash crew was injured; I guess they knew it was going to catch fire because they pumped water on it from a distance and put out the fire.

The first attack on North Vietnam by South Vietnam.

February 9, 1965

Two of our aircraft (245) and (237) were on missions near the town of Dong Hoi in the south of North Vietnam just north of the South Vietnam border. The pictures showed a large staging area around the city. We have a

2pm takeoff for both of those aircraft. Major Musgrove and Captain Cobb and Major Stanfield and Lt. Platt are the crews. When they arrived at the aircraft they told us there was a big air strike in progress at this time in that area in retaliation for North Vietnam and Viet Cong recent attacks on our base in Pleiku. They are going up there to take pictures of the damage but the weather may be a problem except for the in-fra-red cameras.

Only the Navy Aircraft from the Carriers in the South China Sea got through because of bad weather and our aircraft could not get any decent pictures. Of the 49 Navy planes that got through the bad weather, one Navy A-4D D Sky Hawk was shot down by communist ground fire. Our guys said they couldn't get any clear pictures but they said there was a lot of damage and heavy fire and smoke. Our pilots said that none of the aircraft from South Vietnam could make it because of the bad weather but they would be back the next day.

On Monday, after the weather cleared, the Vietnamese Air Force Commander Brig. Gen. Nguyen Cao Ky personally led a raid of 24 A1-H and A1-E South Vietnamese Sky Raider fighter bombers and U.S. Air Force F- 100 super sabers into the same area. We sent 245 into North Vietnam to get pictures now that the weather had cleared. Gen. Ky later said his flight destroyed major portions of three North Vietnamese military camps and left them burning. General Ky identified the villages in the Vinh Linh area as Liem Cong Tay, That Le and Song Song. The three towns are near the frontier and along a route leading toward the border. He said four F- 100s bombed an area just to the north of his target region, reportedly with excellent results. Our RB-57 got some great pictures of the destroyed targets.

In a meeting our Pilots attended, the air Commodore said flak in his area was extremely heavy and that it was clear that the Communists knew they were coming, after the Vietnamese Air Force aborted its mission Sunday because of bad weather.

He said of the 24 Sky Raiders, one Vietnamese Air Force A-1H Sky Raider was hit by antiaircraft fire over the target and crashed near Da Nang airbase on its return flight. The pilot parachuted safely and suffered only a bruised shoulder. Ky said he understood one US plane was hit by flak but that there were no casualties among American personnel. Ky declined to say if there would be more raids on North Vietnam. He said he could spot many casualties on the ground as the planes turned to go home. One of our pilots said that at the meeting Ky was dressed in a black flying suit and lavender scarf and an anti-gravity suit and a 45 automatic pistol strapped to his side. Ky's plane itself had been hit and that a bullet grazed through Ky's flight suit under his arm without hurting him badly.

One of our F102 pilots told us they were flying cover over the strike and they met with no resistance and there were no Mig 17 jet fighters in the area at all.

We learned from our pilots that were at the meeting that seven U.S. Air Force pilots led Monday's air attack on North Vietnam. The pilots said they served as Pathfinders and flak suppressors during the raid meaning they went in first and hit North Vietnamese antiaircraft emplacements. The Americans flew South Vietnam propeller driven A-1H Sky Raider fighter bombers.

The American pilots received the air medal decoration from South Vietnam for their "support" for the raid.

Meanwhile, in Saigon the nation's leader, Lt. Gen. Nguyen Khanh, reporting on the radio and the local paper described the Vietnamese pilots who made the Vinh Linh area raid Monday as "the favorite sons of Vietnam". Khanh said the 24 Vietnamese aircraft participating in the raid had planned their bombing and strafing for Sunday but were forced back because of very bad weather. Supported by US aircraft Ky's A-1-H force returned Monday hitting its targets at 3:30 PM local time. Khanh said the targets, various military installations, were 70% destroyed, and columns of smoke and flames were seen rising from the area. Asked if more raids against North Vietnam were coming, Khanh replied; "The activities of the Vietnamese armed forces will be both timely and to the point". He declined on grounds of military security to say whether more raids were planned.

On Sunday our RB-57 aircraft could not get good photos of the damage because of the weather but on Monday they returned and came back with a lot of good photos for the Generals running this war. I saw the photos when they were developed and they really tore up the countryside up there.

This was the first time the South Vietnamese had attacked the North Vietnamese in this war.

When General Ky and some of his pilots returned to Tan Son Nhut airfield in Saigon I was at work. Six A-1H's came across the field at about 200 mph and when each one of them peeled out to land they did a victory roll which was awesome. They were about 50 feet above the runway and then each one of them went straight up and rolled three times before they turned and came around to land. There was a large crowd waiting for them when they taxied in to park. It was quite a sight; they cheered and hugged each of the pilots, and this man, General Ky, is so loved by his pilots and his troops it's amazing. As I said before Gen. Ky is not only a hero to his South Vietnamese people but also of us Americans. He would later become president of this nation.

February 11 1965

It was reported in this morning's paper because the North Vietnamese have escalated this war; President Johnson directed Sunday to raise the state of military readiness from Defense Condition 4 to Defcon 3. The highest order of readiness is Defcon 1, which a state of war. Next is Defcon 2 or near war. He also commanded "the orderly withdrawal of American dependents from South Vietnam".

The Defense Department reported there are about 600 dependents of military personnel in South Vietnam, plus 150 dependents of civilian employees of the military. In a news conference later in the day Secretary of Defense Robert S McNamara estimated the overall total of dependents at about 1,800, including wives and children of diplomatic, civilian and aid personnel. We sure were sorry to hear about that because we will no longer get to see the pretty American girls at the pool in Saigon.

President Johnson also ordered a Hawk missile air defense battalion to be deployed to Da Nang airfield in the North of South Vietnam and said "other reinforcements, units and personnel may follow".

I sure wish we had some of those Hawk antiaircraft missiles that are being sent to Da Nang down here at Tan Son Nhut because they are judged particularly effective against low-flying planes.

A typical Hawk antiaircraft missile battalion contains 500 to 600 men and either 18 or 24 missile launchers. The Hawk missile so named because it raises high in the air and swoops down on low-flying planes like a hawk is 16 feet long and 14 inches in diameter.

The Hawk missiles plugged a hole in the defenses around Da Nang. There was nothing specifically designed before the Hawks arrived to handle low-flying enemy aircraft before they could get in close to the base.

February 13, 1965

One of our RB-57 aircraft was taking pictures of targets up north near the airbase at Da Nang when they noticed a large group of Viet Cong about 5 miles away moving toward the base. The pilot contacted the authorities there at the base then he hung around to guide the attack aircraft.

He said about 15 min. later here come at least 35 aircraft plus armed and troop carrying helicopters, spotter planes and South Vietnam A-1 H sky raider fighter bombers. They were all coming toward the target he called in.

He said rockets and bombs were exploding all over the place as the Viet Cong troops ran in panic across the open field. He said they watched the attack from a safe altitude as machine guns from the armed choppers swooped 50 feet off the ground skimming the trees and clearing a landing area for the troop ships. He said there were at least 200 or 300 Vietnamese airborne troops, running from the Marine helicopters when they landed to block the fleeing enemy. The pilot said they hung around for a few more minutes took a few more pictures and then headed back to Tan Son Nhut Airbase at Saigon.

We later herd the operation had been a success, 40 to 50 Viet Cong were killed by the bombs and rockets from the A-1 H sky Raiders and their bodies had been carried off by the Viet Cong. One South Vietnamese soldier was killed and 4 others were wounded by machine-gun fire. The only American casualty was an American helicopter pilot wounded slightly in the hand.

Spooky Dudes Show up

February 14 1965.

We were all at a meeting Saturday morning outside of the pilot's operation building with Major Musgrove, when an Air America Caribou aircraft taxied into our parking ramp. Every month or so they would show up in some kind of an aircraft or another that had no markings on it, "no tail number, no Country (no nothing) on the aircraft to identify it". We called them "Spooky Dudes" because they wore no uniforms and would never tell us what they were up to. This time two guys (CIA agents) got out and come over to where we were all standing around. The meeting was over and some of us were having a beer and talking, due to we had no flights that Saturday. They joined in with us and we gave them a couple of beers, but they wouldn't tell us what they were up to. All they would say was Major Musgrove took some pictures for them over in Laos near the Ho Chi Minh trail. They just stopped by to pick them up and see if he would help them out with more pictures they need in a different area.

I am not sure but I think Major Musgrove has some kind of an agreement with them because they would stop and see him about once a month. Major Musgrove had said before he had some people that give him information that the military does not give him. The Major said they were very useful for information where we have no military intelligence people. It makes some of our missions safer. Sgt Smith and I were setting at the picnic table outside the pilots operations building with one of the CIA agents named Bill having a beer. They would only tell us their first names and that they held officer rank in the US Military. Major Stanfield our intelligence officer sat down with us to have a beer and told Bill that they would be in the area they wanted pictures of on Tuesday of next week. He also said that he would relay the message to General Moore, our base commander (that the Major did not share with us). Then they got back in their aircraft and took off "for who knows where".

David Karmes

F-102 Crash (My Big Mistake)

February 15, 1965

Those of us that work in the jet parking area (that the RB 57s started back in 1963), we all work close together. If the guys that work on the RF- 101 Voo Doo's the F-102 Delta Dagger's or the RB- 57s need something we will help each other if we can.

One of the F-102 Delta Dagger interceptors was on a routine mission 20 miles south of the base when he had an engine failure and had to eject out of the aircraft. The pilot was not hurt and was picked up by the South Vietnamese Army. The aircraft crashed at a low angle into a bunch of trees, but it did not catch fire, although there was a lot of damage, it was still all together. They decided they were going to blow it up, but there were some classified electronics on it and they wanted to remove them if possible. They also wanted to send a team out to inspect what was left of the engine to see if they could figure out what went wrong with it.

One of the F-102 crew chiefs, (Joe), who I hang out with occasionally, asked me if I would help him get the black boxes out of that aircraft. He was assigned to get what he could out of the aircraft before they destroyed it. The area the aircraft crashed in is a semi-secure area and was being guarded by South Vietnamese troops. It could be dangerous if there are any Viet Cong in the area. The aircraft was, also, fully armed which makes it dangerous.

I checked in with Sgt. Cogdill and he said it was okay to help them. The next morning we assembled at the Army Huey helicopter parking area. After getting my AR- 15 rifle plus my 45 caliber pistol, we gathered what tools we thought we would need. There were six of us plus the Army helicopter crews, two engine people to check the engine if possible, two armament guys to make the weapons safe and Joe and myself. We had three armed Huey helicopters. In our helicopter there was the pilot and copilot, one Army helicopter mechanic and one Army gunner that manned one of the 50 caliber machine guns mounted at each door. The other two helicopters were fully armed and had two Army door gunners. We flew in formation out to the site and we landed in a clearing about 100 yards from where the F-102 aircraft had crashed. There were 25 South Vietnamese Army troops guarding the aircraft. The two other armed Huey's that were with us went back into the air and patrolled the area to make sure the area was secure, also there were two South Vietnamese A-1 H fighter bombers patrolling the area. When we got to the downed F-102 aircraft, "what a mess", there were parts all over the place. The armament guys kept us away until they made sure the weapons that were still intact on the aircraft were safe. Then Joe and I and the Army mechanic located the electronic black boxes we were after. We removed four of the five we were after but the fifth one was completely destroyed.

We then loaded them into our Huey and were waiting for the others to finish checking what they could of the engine. All of a sudden a mortar shell hit in the trees about 50 yards from our helicopter. There was a huge explosion and dirt and wood was flying all over the place and a piece of a tree hit the tail rotor of our helicopter and damaged it, making it unable to fly so we could not leave the area. Then another mortar came in about 100 yards away and did no damage except for our ear drums. When that one hit, we were all looking for cover so we dove into a low area near our damaged helicopter. Then another came in no less than 30 ft from where we took cover but it didn't go off, there was just a thud as it hit and it buried itself in the ground. If that mortar would have exploded it most likely would have killed all of us. The only thing I could think about was, what am I doing here and yes I was really scared. I knew the next one was going to be right on us. I think GOD was protecting us because the next one never came. Then we could hear gunfire coming from some of the South Vietnamese troops that were guarding the F-102 off in the distance, approximately half a mile away. The other two helicopters attacked an area approximately 1 mile away where the mortars were coming from. The South Vietnamese A-1H fighter bombers were coming right over our heads firing rockets from the rocket pods under their wings. They circled around and came back right over our heads again and this time they dropped napalm bombs. We could hear a huge fire fight going on when the armed Huey's and the A-1 Hs would open up, strafing the area with their guns. There was a huge column of smoke coming up from the napalm bombs, then everything was quiet, no mortars coming in at us and no gunfire. The A-1Hs were circling overhead, then the other 2 Huey's landed and we scrambled aboard them, except for the Army crew of our helicopter, they stayed behind with their helicopter. We didn't even grab our AR-15s or the black boxes that were on our damaged helicopter, we just wanted out of there. Three more Huey helicopters appeared and they started patrolling the area.

The guys in our helicopter said there were about 100 Viet Cong moving toward the crash site, although the main bunch were more than a couple of miles away, except for some Viet Cong patrols that were closer. Those were the ones that the South Vietnamese were shooting at. The helicopter that I was in had been hit by ground fire and was leaking fuel all the way back to Ton Son Nhut airfield, but we didn't know it until we landed. I know that GOD was with me in that, too. It could have caught fire or exploded at any time. We found out later they repaired the damaged Huey and flew it back to the base with our black boxes, our AR 15's and our tools.

What a big mistake on my part, volunteering for that mission. When that first mortar hit all we could think about was finding cover. When the one that hit right next to us within 30 feet that didn't explode, that really scared me because I figured the next one (that never happened) would get us. But the guys in the Hueys and the A-1's hit the Viet Cong where the mortars were coming from and they stopped coming in. The only damage they caused to our Huey was that piece of wood that hit the tail rotor.

I had no business being out there in the jungle without combat training. The next day the Army brought our weapons, the black boxes and our tools over. The Army helicopter mechanic that helped us said that we did real well; except the next time to grab your weapon before you look for cover. We told him, you guys do a good job and there will be no next time for us. We did get four of the five black boxes we were after, plus the guys checking the engine found the remains of a large bird in it that caused the engine to fail.

When I was telling the guys at work what had happened they thought it was funny, but I let them know I didn't think it was funny at all. Although I was not in combat in Vietnam, there were several times when the Viet Cong could have gotten me but I know now that GOD was protecting me for another reason.

More Chinese Jets

Wednesday Feb. 15 1965

I arrived at work that afternoon just as Major Mc Ginnes and Captain Young were climbing out of (237). They had just returned from a mission over North Viet Nam near the China border. Just then the base commander's staff car showed up and Major Mc Ginnes jumped in and they took off. We asked Capt. Young what was going on, and he said they took pictures of over 100 Chinese jet aircraft located on Chinese airfields near the border of North Vietnam and Major McGinnis was ordered to report to General Moore immediately before the pictures are even developed.

    Capt. Young said that their target was two Chinese bases just north of the North Vietnam border. He said they flew along the border staying out of Chinese air space and when they saw all of the Jets parked at those basis that were next to the border, they took the pictures and then high tailed it out of there at treetop level so the Chinese radar could not see them. He also said there were several Chinese Mig Jet fighters in the area but they did not see them because they were flying so low just above treetops. He said that if those Chinese jets had seen them they probably would not have made it back to the base. The next day Major Musgrove convened a special meeting that we all attended that showed the classified pictures of hundreds of Chinese Jets parked at those bases just north of the North Vietnam border in China. After that meeting, I am not sure but I think that our B- 57's were not allowed to go that far north near the Chinese border in the daytime without jet fighter cover from F- 100, F- 102 or Navy fighter jets. Most of those targets now were assigned to the RF- 101's because they were so much faster than any Chinese jet. At night we can go almost anywhere we want and get some great pictures with our infrared cameras. Matter of fact, the next night Major Musgrove and Captain Cobb took 237 (because it has upgraded infrared cameras compared to 243 or 245) back up there for two hours and rode around taking pictures like they owned the place.

We later learned that Nationalist Chinese intelligence sources said that Communist China have sent nearly 150 jet aircraft to airfields near the border of North Vietnam. They said its sources were claiming the communist have sent a total of "nine squadrons" or 144 aircraft to airfields in its border provinces.

Nationalist Air Force sources said nine squadrons would amount to that number, and the figure of 16 aircraft per squadron.

They said its sources claimed the aircraft would be able to reach any target in Vietnam from those airfields. They also said the Chinese have completed a rail and road transportation network that would enable them to move an estimated 70,000 troops or 14,000 tons of supplies into Vietnam daily.

Another Coup

Friday, February 16, 1965, oh boy here we go again another Coup.

We had been hearing rumors all morning that something was happening in Saigon. I was working when it all started and I had just climbed up on the wing of my airplane to check the fuel during the preflight inspection. It was 4pm and my aircraft had a 5pm takeoff, the pilots had not shown up yet at the operations building. I looked up and there was a South Vietnamese tank coming down the parking ramp and weaving between the RF- 101's parked in the middle of the ramp, going like hell. My aircraft was parked in the first sandbag revetment next to the turnoff to the taxiway and when the tank passed, it was so close to the front of my aircraft it hit the end of the sand bag revetment as it turned to go to the taxiway. I could also see there were several tanks going out onto the main runway.

Then, all of a sudden, here came an A-1H Sky Raider coming down the taxiway going wide open on takeoff. The tank that had been coming down the ramp went out onto the taxiway just as the A-1H left the ground and went right over the top of the tank and then banked to the right and came right over the top of me and just cleared the air Vietnam hangers as he took off. Then about 200 South Vietnamese Army troops came in and completely surrounded the jet parking area. I jumped down off of my aircraft just as a South Vietnamese officer came over and told us to take cover it looks like there was going to be some shooting pretty soon.

It seems that the Army was trying to take control of the government and the Army took over the whole Tan Son Nhut airbase and most of Saigon.

They would not let anything land or take off so they put their tanks out on the runway and the taxiway's. We all gathered at the maintenance trailer to try to figure out what we were going to do. About 15 or 20 minutes later 15 A-1 H skyraiders flew over the base in formation, they have come down from Bien Hoa airbase with bombs, rockets and guns and was buzzing the Army troops trying to make them leave the base. The South Vietnamese Air Force led by our hero General Ky was not going to let the rebel troops take over the base or the Government. General Ky was the one that took off in his A1-H on the taxiway. We got a call in the trailer from the US Air Force Command post, and they said they wanted someone to get on our truck radio and let them know everything that was happening in our area. The Vietnamese Army would not let anyone get to the jet parking area and would not let us out.

It seems I am working with a bunch of chickens; none of them would get out in the truck on the radio so I volunteered. I went out on the flight line with the truck and parked between two sandbag revetments next to my aircraft. There were 200 Vietnamese Army troops; about one hundred yards away and eight A-1 H sky Raiders flying around ordering the Army Rebels to leave. I parked the truck so I could see down the flight line parking ramp in both directions. Both sides looked like they were ready to fire back just as soon as one side fired on the other. I had to call the command Post every time a tank or a bunch of troops moved. I had to tell them which way they were headed and how many. It got kind of hairy there for a while, those A-1 H's would come in low and I mean real low, so low that when they would go over me I could feel the wind that it made. A South Vietnamese army Jeep pulled up next to my truck and a Major got out. He came over to the truck and asked me why I wasn't with the other guy's hiding in a sand bag revetment. I told him the truth that I was reporting to our Command post on what he and his troops were doing on the truck radio. It really pissed me off, so I asked him what the hell he and his troops were doing. I told him, you see my aircraft here; it should be in the air right now gathering intelligence to protect your troops but you won't let my pilots in here to fly. I pointed over toward the F-102s and said, you see those aircraft, if this base is attacked by the North Vietnamese they will not be able to take off to protect us because you have the runway blocked by your tanks. He backed off, looked at me and got back in his jeep and drove away. This went on for three hours; those tanks going up and down the flight line and the A-1Hs flying low right over my head. Just as it was getting dark that South Vietnamese Major showed up again and this time he had two troops with him. I figured I was in big trouble now. They got out of the jeep and one of the troops had a bucket and handed it to me. In it was some still warm fried rice and chicken, then the Major said they figured I would be hungry so they brought me some food. It was really good, too, probably the best I have ever had. Then he told me to let Air Force Command know that he would protect the American troops and our aircraft in this area and he did not agree with his Commanders. I then wrote his name down because I could not pronounce it and reported his name and what he said to Air Force Command. Not one shot was fired though in the two day's we stayed there on the flight line even though I thought all hell was going to break loose. Those Army troops had their guns pointed at the A-1H aircraft every time they would fly over and followed them until they were out of range. The South Vietnamese Air Force prevailed and they locked up the Army General that started the whole thing and all the troops went back to fighting the Viet Cong instead of each other.

The attempt by Rebel Army troops and Marines to overthrow the government of South Vietnams president Lt. General Nguyen Khanh collapsed in less than 24 hours. Saigon radio, which had been in rebel hands, announced early Saturday it was returning to normal control and it ceased broadcasting rebel communiqués.

The Radio station reported the collapse of the coup came without bloodshed. The rebels apparently surrendered the radio station after 2000 loyalist troops began marching into the city.

The collapse of the rebellion came only hours before Vietnam's Air Force Commander Vice Air Marshal Nguyen Cao Ky threatened to bomb rebel positions in the city. The Air Force chief warned the rebel leader, Brig. Gen, Lam Van Phat to evacuate Saigon's Tan Son Nhut airbase or face bombing by loyal airman.

We later learned the rebel leader was apparently backed also by a Regiment of the 25th infantry division stationed near Saigon. Some Marines and Air Force units also were on the Rebel side. The South Vietnam Navy stayed neutral, its ships pulled out of Saigon and dropped anchor 7 miles down the river. General Khanh escaped early in the coup and reached Cape St Jacques, on the coast from where he telephoned American Generals that he had three paratroop battalions ready to march on Saigon. General Khanh apparently slipped away just as the rebel tanks rumbled up to his Saigon residence. General Ky also managed to escape from Ton Son Nhut air base in an A-1H fighter bomber (the one that went over me) and he rallied his men at the Bien Hoa airbase outside Saigon for action against the rebels in the capital.

I sure do wish these people would make up their minds who they want to rule this place. I worry more about these coups than I do the Viet Cong.

General Moore, the base commander, came down to the flight line and thanked us for the great job we did reporting what was going on to Air Force Command. I was not there when he came down but the guys told him I was the one in the truck. I wonder what he thought of the lowest ranking man that was in the truck reporting, I am sure they did not tell him what chickens they were.

Two days later Lt. General Nguyen Khanh resigned his position as leader and commander in chief of the Republic of Vietnam's Armed Forces. He was replaced by General Nguyen Minh. Kahanh, whose ouster was announced to the nation, was expected to be brought back to the capital from Vung Tau 40 miles from Saigon where he had fled. On Tuesday he resigned his post formally and made arrangements for his departure. General Khanh was later appointed ambassador at large for the country of South Vietnam. The radio reported that General Khanh flew to Saigon with US Army Col. Jasper Wilson, a friend of Khanh, who has been keeping an eye on the former commander to make sure no attempts were made on his life. Following Khanh's transfer ceremony onThursday he is scheduled to go immediately to Saigon airport to board a special flight to Hong Kong where he is reported to stay several days.

General Khanh had been staying at his palace in Dalat since Sunday night when he was notified that his staff had ousted him by a no-confidence vote. He will be taking his family with him out of Vietnam to assume his new formal post as ambassador without portfolio. His first mission will be to present fresh evidence of Viet Cong infiltration to the United Nations. In effect, however, he will be a political exile like many others who have been given an overseas post to get them out of Vietnam honorably. Most of us were sorry to see him go; he was a good leader and did many great things for South Vietnam.

February 18, 1965

In route to a target along the coast 243 spotted a large ship that was partially camouflaged just off shore.

They didn't have time to investigate so they contacted a helicopter that was flying below them to check it out.

What they found was a cargo ship of an estimated 100 ton capacity, carefully camouflaged and moored just off shore along the coast. That same day we sent 243 back to take pictures of the attack on that ship. Our Pilots told us that when the A-1H Fighter planes approached the vessel, they met machine- gun fire from guns on the deck of the ship and from the shore as well.

The ship was sunk in shallow water and the pictures that 243 took showed a huge cargo of arms, ammunition and other supplies that were already on the shore. We later learned that the supplies delivered by the ship- thousands of weapons and more than 1 million rounds of ammunition were almost all of communist origin. Most were from communist China and Czechoslovakia, as well as North Vietnam. At least 100 tons of military supplies were discovered on shore near the ship.

The base paper reported when they inspected the ship they found it was fairly new and had been made in Communist China. Documents aboard the ship included three North Vietnamese nautical charts one of the Haiphong areas and one of Hong Gay, both in North Vietnam and one of the Tra Vinh areas of South Vietnam. The military health records of North Vietnamese soldiers were found. One man had a political history sheet showing he was a member of the 338th division of the North Vietnamese Army.

It looks like things here are becoming more and more dangerous with more North Vietnam regular troops entering South Vietnam plus the new weapons from China. We have to be extremely careful when we go to town not to gather in groups or go into certain areas.

Here is an excerpt from a U.S. White Paper on Vietnam entitled Greater Violence.

Today the war in Vietnam has reached new levels of intensity. The elaborate effort by the communist regime in North Vietnam to conquer the South has grown not diminished. Military men, technicians, political organizers, propagandists and secret agents have been infiltrating into the Republic of Vietnam from the north in growing numbers.

The government in Saigon has undertaken vigorous action to meet the new threat. The United States and other free countries have increased their assistance to the Vietnamese government and people.

It has been apparent for years that the regime in Hanoi is conducting a campaign of conquest in South Vietnam. The government in Saigon and the government in the United States both hoped that the danger could be met within South Vietnam itself. The hope that any widening of the conflict might be avoided was stated frequently. The leaders in Hanoi choose to respond with greater violence. They apparently interpreted restraint as indicating a lack of will. Their efforts were pressed with greater vigor and armed attacks and incidents of terror multiplied.

Clearly the restraint of the past was not providing adequately for the defense of South Vietnam against Hanoi's open aggression. It was mutually agreed between the governments of the Republic of Vietnam and the United States that further means for providing for South Vietnam's defense were required. Therefore, air strikes have been made against some of the military assembly points in North Vietnam and supply bases from which North Vietnam was conducting its aggression against the South. These strikes constitute a limited response fitted to the aggression that produced them.

Until the regime in Hanoi decides to halt its intervention in the South or until effective steps are taken to maintain peace and security in the area, the governments of South Vietnam and the United States will continue necessary measures of defense against the communist armed aggression coming from North Vietnam.

CHAPTER 10

MARCH 1965

U. S. Jets in combat for the first time in South Vietnam

March 1 1965

We have a 2 PM takeoff time for aircraft 245 and when the pilots arrived at the aircraft they told us that the first strike on the Viet Cong in South Vietnam by our B-57's from Bien Hoa was under way and they were off to take pictures of the damage. After they took off, we could hear the bombs going off in the distance south of Saigon and when they returned they said that the B-57's did a lot of damage and they had some really good pictures that we could look at later.

The United States disclosed that US jets piloted by Americans have gone into combat action in the Republic of South Vietnam for the first time.

A US spokesman said twin jet B-57B bombers first went into action against communist Viet Cong forces in Phouc Tuy Province, about 40 miles Southeast of Saigon. The B-57's from Bien Hoa and American F-100 jet fighter aircraft from Da Nang airfield in the North blasted the communist to help rescue Vietnamese troops trapped by a Viet Cong offensive.

US military spokesman said the twin jet Canberra bombers dropped 59 loads of bombs Thursday and Friday where the communist have staged a massive buildup of regular forces in the past few months. Our pilots reported as many as 4000 communist troops operating in the province.

We had previously used our B-57s in a series of retaliatory airstrikes against communist North Vietnam. But inside South Vietnam US jets had been limited to reconnaissance only by our RB-57 and RF-101 aircraft. Until the present; American aerial combat assistance to the government of South Vietnam has generally been limited to the use of WW-2 propeller driven aircraft plus the versatile HU-1B (Huey) helicopters.

In disclosing the use of the jet aircraft a US Embassy spokesman said at the request of the government of South Vietnam, US Air Force F- 100 and B- 57 jet aircraft from Bien Hoa and Da Nang participated in the combined air strike.

February 26, 1965

We finally got the okay to send 55-4245 back to General Dynamics in Fort Worth to install the new updates on it. I don't remember who the lucky crew was but I think it probably was Major McGinnis and Captain Young. When it returns we will send 243 for the new updates.

We had the ABC television news people working with one of our aircraft yesterday and today. Now that we are using B-57s here in South Vietnam, I guess they figured the people back in the States would like to know a little bit about them. I don't know why they picked our aircraft because we don't carry any bombs or guns. All we can do is take pictures. I thought it was pretty funny myself; it took them two hours just to shoot 5 min. worth of film.

Yesterday they shot film of one of our pilots showing each of his survival gear. Today they shot pictures of a guy standing in front of my airplane and was telling about the bomb load and guns on the B-57 plus other things about the aircraft. They sure did waste a bunch of film. They would shoot it once then decided it wasn't quite right, so they would do it all over again; they did this for two hours straight. I asked them why they didn't go up to Bien Hoa airbase where the armed B-57s were to do their shoot. They said it was dangerous up there and our aircraft at least looked like a real B-57 so they would stay here where it was safe. What a bunch of wusses.

David Karmes

Big Snake

March 4, 1965

I arrived at work early and was going to play some horseshoes with the guys until time to go to work. I noticed a bunch of guys over by the pilots operation building looking into a ditch that run toward the Air Vietnam hangers. I walked over to see what they were looking at. When I looked down in the ditch there was a big ole snake just laying there looking up at us. It was about four or five feet long and did not look very dangerous, he was just laying there minding his own business. A few minutes later a South Vietnamese security guard from the Air Vietnam hanger wandered over to see what we were looking at.

When he saw the snake he went off like a bomb hollering at us in Vietnamese. He didn't speak a word of English but we knew we needed to get away from that snake. Then he ran over to a guard shack near the hanger where there was a phone. A few minutes later the Vietnamese Military Police showed up and shot the snake with an AR-15 carbine

It turned out to be a King Cobra snake, you know the kind that rise up and flatten their head and can spit venom at you. And some of those guys were talking about grabbing it by the tail and yanking it out of the ditch. They sure were glad that guard showed up.

March 6, 1965

Saturday morning Major Musgrove called a meeting of all of the troops and said that the Generals running this war are telling him they wanted our operation to pack up and move up north to Da Nang airbase where most of the action is going on at this time. They said things are getting real quiet around Saigon but things are real hot up North and that's where they need us right now. All the Viet Cong were moving north and they are planning on something happening up there around Da Nang, and that's where we will be going if we do go. Da Nang is 375 miles North of Saigon and about 20 miles south of the 17th parallel. The 17th parallel is the border between North and South Vietnam. Two days later all hell broke loose down in the Mekong Delta South of Saigon so they decided we better stay where we were, besides it would take weeks just to move all of our equipment and Da Nang didn't even have a place to put us. We would have to work out of tents and stay in tents and we all complained vehemently. If the Viet Cong are going up there we sure didn't want to be there. In the meeting we found out president Johnson is sending 2000 Marines to guard the Da Nang airbase which would've been okay if we went there we maybe would've been safer than here in Saigon. Although it's not safe anywhere in this country no matter how many of our troops there are. So instead of our RB-57s going up north they sent six of our RF- 101s there to take care of those targets on a temporary basis, they will be back in a few weeks.

F-4C Phantom Jets Arrive in South East Asia

Major Musgrove was telling us the president is sending the new Air Force F-4C Phantom tactical jet fighter to South East Asia. He is sending a lot more equipment, arms and a lot more troops into South Vietnam, this war sure looks like it's going to escalate.

Here is what we learned a few days later, a squadron of the Air Force's newest and fastest tactical jet fighter the F-4C Phantom will be assigned to the Philippines to strengthen American and Filipino air defenses. The F-4 C's will replace a part of the Air Force's F-102 jet interceptor force now stationed at Clark Air Force Base. The F- 102s will be returned to the US.

The U.S Air Force F-4C squadron will be assigned to the Philippines on a 90 day rotational basis. At the end of the 90 day period the aircraft will remain in the Philippines but the personnel involved will be replaced from another squadron in the US.

The F-4 C is capable of flying at 1600 m.p.h plus, at altitudes exceeding 57,000 feet. The jet is manned by a crew of two and has a range of more than 2000 miles without in-flight refueling. It can carry twice the bomb payload of a World War II B-17 heavy bomber. We sure were glad to hear that and we hope they will send some of them over here plus the RF-101 drivers would like to see if they are as fast as they say they are.

237 in Trouble

March 8, 1965

Monday night Chuck Burton and I are working and we had sent two aircraft 237 and 243 down to the Mekong Delta to take pictures of targets along the canals there. About nine o'clock that evening base operations called us on the radio and said that 237 had been hit and was in trouble and that it was coming in on emergency. We called Sgt. Cogdill and told him 237 had been hit and was coming in on emergency and we were going to need some help. Then the fire trucks were heading out to the runway. A few minutes later 243 and 237 flew in formation low over the flight line right over our heads. Because it was dark we could not see anything wrong with the aircraft except that it was not on fire. The tower couldn't see anything either so 243 peeled off and come around and landed first just in case 237 could not make it and crashed on the runway and blocked it. Then 237 come around and landed without any problems. When 237 taxied in there were two big holes in it. They were hit with armor piercing bullets, those are the ones that explode when they hit. There was a big hole in the left wing, and one in the bottom of the aircraft. The one in the wing was not real bad but the one in the bottom hit in the bomb bay where the camera equipment is located and they estimate it did around $300,000 worth of damage to the camera equipment. No one was hurt and the aircraft made it back okay but they sure did a lot of damage. If that bullet had hit 5 feet further forward it would have come right into the cockpit and we probably would have lost the aircraft and possibly the crew. The one that hit the wing had come real close to the fuel tank and had it hit the tank we surely would've lost the aircraft. I have the highest respect for our pilots, they are the bravest men that are in this country. We patched up the aircraft as best we could and sent it over to the Philippines for major repair, they put in all new camera equipment and fixed it up real nice and sent it back to us in 4 days. That's how important our aircraft are in this war, we even have top priority in the Philippines.

The Lazy Dog Bomb

We have been taking a lot of small arms hits and this last episode when 237 was hit with armor piercing bullets prompted the installation of a weapon on our aircraft. When they would fly over the canals down in the Mekong Delta or a clearing in the jungle the Viet Cong knew we were not armed and would run out and shoot at the aircraft with whatever they had. Major Musgrove, I believe it was him, came up with a simple weapon. It was a pod installed under the wing that looked like a bomb with electric doors on it and was filled by hand with hundreds of Lazy Dog Bombs.

Here is what I could find out about the Lazy Dog Bomb in my research.

Developed as an anti-personnel weapon during the 1950s, Lazy Dog missiles were made from solid steel with stabilizing fins. Early lazy dogs were made from forged steel, later designs were of lath- turned steel. The Lazy Dog "bombs" (sometimes called red dot bombs or yellow dog bombs) were small unguided kinetic missiles, each measuring 1.75 inches in length. They are one half inch in diameter, and weigh 207 grains, or about 0.7 of an ounce. The weapons were designed to be disbursed over the battle field with Mark 44 cluster adapters. Lazy dog bombs were technically not bombs because they used no explosive, but were in many ways equally destructive.

The lazy dog bombs were descended from projectiles of almost identical design and appearance that were originally developed in as early as 1941. The Korean War- era and Vietnam war- era "lazy dog" was further developed tested and deployed into the 1950s and 1960s.

Lazy dog projectiles were usable with almost any kind of flying vehicle. They could be hurled from buckets, dropped by hand, thrown in their small shipping bags made of paper, or shoveled out of the back of a C-1 23 aircraft flying over the enemy.

In the early years of US involvement in Vietnam, helicopter crewman literally threw bucket loads of them out of the chopper's door while flying at speed over enemy positions. They could also be dropped from fixed wing cargo planes or thrown from small aircraft. Each micro-missile was fin stabilized and capable of attaining the terminal velocity of 700 feet per second which produced penetrating power equivalent to between a 45 caliber slug and a 30 caliber carbine.

The rationale for using lazy dogs in the Viet Nam war was because they were highly effective against enemy troops hidden beneath the jungle canopy. The munitions were also cheap and easy to scatter over large areas. Like many other weapons, however, their effects were often gruesome and indiscriminate. Lazy dog projectiles were also referred to by other names such as "lawn darts" or "buzz bombs" because of their similar shape to both of those objects. Regardless of how they were released into the air, each "lazy dog" projectile developed an incredible amount of kinetic energy as it fell, penetrating nearly any material on hitting the ground. Some reports say that their speeds often exceeded 500 mph before impact. When they were released there was nowhere to hide, they would even penetrate 9 inches of concrete when released from 3000 feet.

March 15, 1965

I arrived at work on the flight line about 4 PM for a 5PM take off of 245. The day shift had already done the preflight inspection on the aircraft and there was a crowd of people around it. They had just finished installing our new weapon on 245 and everybody was checking it out. It just looked like a bomb hanging there under the wing. When the pilots arrived at the aircraft Major Stanfield and LT. Platt were the air crew. I accompanied Major Stanfield on his (walk around inspection) of the aircraft and when he got to the weapon he checked it over real good. He said there was a large buildup of North Vietnamese and Viet Cong about 30 miles North of Saigon and their target was in that area and he was hoping to use that new weapon. I helped the pilots get strapped in and Major Stanfield started the engines, taxied out and took off with no problem. About 7 PM we were waiting for 245 to return from the mission and a bunch of people showed up and they said that major Stanfield had called in on the radio and said that he had used the weapon and they were waiting to see what had happened. Then a few minutes later here come 245 real low going about 200 miles an hour (well maybe not quite that fast) across the field and right down the runway. Then he went straight up in the air and did a victory roll like the A-1H Sky Raiders do after a successful airstrike and then he came around turned down wind and came around and landed. He taxied in and stopped in the middle of the ramp and shut down the engines and opened the canopy. I went around and put the landing gear safety pins in and came around and put the ladder up, climbed up and told him that was the most awesome victory roll I had ever seen and I've seen a lot of them. He looked up at me with this huge grin on his face and said wait till you see the pictures we took. The crew got out of the aircraft and told us what had happened.

He said that when they passed over a clearing in the jungle there must have been 100 Viet Cong come running out into the open. They started firing every weapon they had at them. (They did take some hits in the tail horizontal stabilizer but did little damage). He said they peeled off to get away from the gun fire and went up to altitude turned around and came back. Those Viet Cong were still in that clearing getting ready to fire at them again, he said he nosed the aircraft down and pointed the nose toward the clearing and released the weapon. He said they immediately turned to the right and climbed back up to altitude. He didn't know if he hit that clearing or even if anything happened. But when they flew back over (up out of range) they said there were bodies lying all over the place and they did get some good pictures

I didn't get to see the pictures and I am glad I didn't, they said they were extremely gruesome with dead and wounded lying all over the clearing. The first week they used the weapon they counted on the pictures 60 dead or wounded. I'm not sure how often they used that weapon because after that first week the pilots didn't talk much about when they did or didn't use it. I do know that the armament people kept the pod full at all times.

March 21, 1965

I have the day off today and one of my friends that works on the RF-101s suggested we grab a six pack of beer and go down to the flight line. He said there is a strong cross wind blowing across the runway and we could just lie up on the sand bag revetment and watch the aircraft land in that cross wind which can be very interesting. I didn't have anything to do that afternoon so I said sounds like a good idea, "let's go" maybe we can play a little horse shoes also. When we got down there some of the guys from the F-102 bunch were already playing so we grabbed a couple of beers out of our cooler. We took off our shirts to get a little sun and jumped up on the sandbags to watch the airplanes land. Just as we got comfortable we could see off in the distance a Pan American Boeing 707 that was coming in with a full load of new troops on our end of the runway. As he got closer we could see that he was having a real hard time with the cross wind, the aircraft was going all over the place. When he crossed the end of the runway near us you could see the right wing tip going way up and then way down. He landed on the right outboard engine, he really banged it good on the runway and there was a loud boom and sparks were flying everywhere. He caught himself and put the airplane back on the landing gear and got the aircraft back under control. It seems that engine wasn't made to land a big Boeing 707 aircraft on. Sparks and parts and pieces were flying everywhere off of that engine and then it caught fire. The fire department rushed out there onto the runway after the aircraft stopped and put the fire out real quickly. He taxied in to the Saigon air terminal and unloaded his shaking troops.

You won't believe what they did next; this was amazing. They don't have any engines here in Vietnam for this aircraft so they took the engine off and streamlined the wing with sheet metal that the hole for the engine mounts left. A few days later they flew it to the Philippines on three engines. Did it ever look funny when they took off, the pilot had to give it full left rudder to keep it on the runway because on the left wing there were two engines pushing the aircraft and on the right wing there was only one engine. It sort of makes the aircraft want to turn to the right but he made it off okay and I guess he made it to the Philippines okay. I hate to see those airplanes get tore up because that is what is going to take me home to my beautiful loving wife in a couple of months. That was enough excitement for the day so we went up to the airman's club and had a few beers.

March 26, 1965

We have a 5pm takeoff of 249, when the air crew showed up they said they were headed up North to take some pictures of an island that was under attack at this minute. On the ship that was sunk last month just off the coast of South Vietnam, they had found paperwork on where the ship had gone through a base on that island. A few days earlier 237 had flown over the island and the pictures showed a large base and a lot of ships around it.

When 249 returned the pilots said that all hell was breaking loose around that island and when they flew over to take pictures they think they took several hits and for us to check the aircraft over real close. Sure enough we found five bullet holes in the aircraft, one in each wing and three in the tail, all of them were minor and did little damage. I called the sheet metal guys down and they patched it up. Those guys are getting pretty good at that, of course we are giving them plenty of work.

Here is the report that was in the paper of that raid.

Twenty-four A-1H South Vietnamese Air Force fighter bombers supported by American jets attacked and destroyed a North Vietnamese island base Sunday, including a radar warning system and port facilities that reportedly handled all the ships that have infiltrated munitions to the Republic of South Vietnam.

All the Vietnamese aircraft got back safely, although several had bullet holes. Neither American nor Vietnamese spokesman would say whether any American planes were downed. The US Jets reportedly went along to suppress flak that might come from the island known in English as "Tiger Island". The US Jets did not fly out of Da Nang and it was presumed that they had taken off from aircraft carriers of the seventh Fleet.

South Vietnamese Air Force commander Brig. Gen. Nguyen Cao Ky said all of the targets on the island 18 miles north of the 17th parallel had been 100% destroyed. At least two American Colonels flew Sky Raiders with Ky's flight and American jets flew "flak suppression". Flak suppression missions involve attacks against anti-aircraft installations in target areas to protect the bombers. He said the Sky Raiders hit some vessels docked around the island and their crews could clearly be seen scrambling for cover and plunging into the sea.

Our pictures from 249 showed the island installations included 49 automatic gun positions, 12 heavier gun positions, a control reconnaissance center, (presumably a radar system) and "many depots and barracks".

During the past month, North Vietnamese authorities reportedly have prohibited all fishing boats from coming near the island within more than 10 miles a spokesman said. The spokesman said 60 tons of ordnance bombs and rockets had been fired at the island, making it one of the smaller raids so far. In the most recent Vietnamese raid on Quang Khe, 80 tons were dropped. Vietnamese and American spokesman said the Tiger Island raid was the only one made on North Vietnamese soil on Sunday. A spokesman said the island was part of the 4th North Vietnamese naval Group. He said the secret munitions ship sunk and captured on the republic of South Vietnams coast last month had passed through the base.

General Ky added that the Air Force would probably attack the island again if there were any attempts to rebuild installations there. The island is about one square mile in area.

David Karmes

United States Embassy Bombed

Tuesday March 30, 1965

Tuesday morning Chuck Burton and I were in Saigon at a shop picking up some pictures we just had developed. We were heading toward one of the base shuttle bus stops near the U.S. Embassy. It is the nearest to where we were to catch the Air Force shuttle bus to head back to the base. We were walking toward the embassy about eight blocks away when the bomb went off. It was a massive explosion of over 200 pounds of plastic explosive that was set off at the front of the U.S. Embassy. There was a flash of light then I could see the shock wave coming down the street at the speed of sound breaking windows in the buildings on both sides of the street. I turned around and bent over when it hit and it knocked Chuck right to the ground. Then glass was breaking out of the windows of the buildings all around us and it about broke our eardrums and we were 8 blocks away.

When we figured out what was going on we could see smoke coming from the Embassy. We did not know what we should do, and then we decided that we needed to see if we could help. We headed up the street making our way among all the debris that was all over the street. When we arrived at the embassy we helped put people into anything that would move to haul them off to the hospital. There were wounded and dead people lying all over the place plus some with only minor injuries.

When everyone was attended to and sent to a hospital we went over to the Naval Hospital and gave blood. There was only one American killed so far, a woman who was engaged to one of our friends here. They were planning on getting married as soon as they got back to the states next July. Chuck took some pictures but I just couldn't. I did not need anything to remind me of that. There were also other Americans hurt that may not make it. Deputy Ambassador Alexis Johnson was inside the American Embassy when the blast tore through the building. He was cut by flying debris but was not seriously hurt and he had come out of the building and was helping us put injured people in the ambulances or cars and taxies or whatever we could find.

The blast was heard throughout the city and like I said it about broke our eardrums and we were several blocks away. The explosion rocked all of downtown Saigon and some buildings are believed to have collapsed as far as two blocks away from the embassy. Several hundred Embassy officials and employees work in the five-story concrete building. The street outside the embassy was a bloody mass of broken bodies when Chuck and I got there.

A U.S. Army officer and an American secretary in the building were killed raising the toll to two Americans and 15 Vietnamese dead. At least 45 Americans and 106 Vietnamese were injured when the Viet Cong terrorist set off an estimated 250 pounds of explosives in a car stopped besides the embassy.

The American secretary killed was identified as Barbara A. Robbins, 21 of Denver Colorado. The officer was not identified and there were no details of his death. The Vietnamese dead included one terrorist who participated in the bombing. The other, carrying a 45 pistol was shot by a policeman just before the bomb went off and was in serious condition. There were about 28 other casualties among non-American foreigners. Many of them were strolling on the street when the massive charge went off at 10:55 AM. Seven of the injured Americans including a woman secretary were in serious condition. A total of seven, some with eye injuries from flying glass were flown to Clark Air Force Base in the Philippines for special treatment.

The blast punched a gaping hole in the five-story concrete Embassy. It shattered every window in the building and dug an enormous crater in the street. Flames and smoke, it looked like to us, were at least 300 feet into the air maybe more. The bomb was planted in a French made sedan which drew up to the embassy and stopped. The Vietnamese policeman on duty told the driver to move on, but he said that he was having engine trouble.

About that time, a motorcycle pulled up and the driver leaped from the car onto the back of it. The policeman reached for his gun and fired at them as they sped away and the men on the motorcycle returned the fire. The policeman was killed, then another policeman wounded the motorcycle driver, dropping him to the pavement. The man still on the motorcycle and several policemen were believed killed in the blast.

That was probably the worst thing that happened to me while I was in Vietnam. All those dead and injured people were a terrible thing to experience.

CHAPTER 11

APRIL 1965

Major Musgrove's 100th Combat mission

I am not quite sure of the exact date of this because for some reason I did not write home about this but because of the pictures I took I do remember Major Musgrove's 100th combat mission.

Major Musgrove returning from his 100th combat mission Captain Cobb is in the back seat

We believe that our Major Musgrove was the first pilot in the Vietnam War to fly 100 combat missions. Each reconnaissance mission was considered a combat mission and it surly was and is very dangerous. All the people running this war on the base came out to welcome him back when he landed including the base commander, General Moore.

April 1, 1965

We just got word that 245 is due back from the states sometime toward the end of April. They say they have painted it black and all of the new radar equipment and upgraded camera equipment is installed on it. I can't wait to see what it looks like. When it gets here 243 is leaving for the states to get all of the new equipment on it and it also will be painted black. That aircraft I will never see again as I will be gone when it gets back.

Also it was announced on Monday that a load of Sky Raider fighter bombers were unloaded Monday from the U.S. Navy converted aircraft carrier Breton. The Sky Raiders will be assigned to the Vietnamese Air Force to beef up its overall strength and to replace the many losses recently.

April 2, 1965

Chuck Burton and I have 2 flights tonight 249 and 243 will takeoff together. And when the pilots arrived for the takeoff they said they will be flying in formation with several B 57B's from Bien Hoe airfield. They will be going up north into North Vietnam to attack a jet air base and they will take pictures as the attack is underway. They took off in formation and circled around the field and in a few minutes here come 5 armed B-57Bs and our 2 RB- 57Es in formation over the field, then they turned and went north.

When they returned about three hours later the pilot's told us what happened. They said it was the first attack directed against any North Vietnamese jet air base. He said there were about 40 aircraft involved including U.S. Navy Jets from the aircraft carriers offshore. Navy F-8 Crusaders and American B- 57's went in first and knocked out the communist antiaircraft guns ringing the base. Then about 24 South Vietnamese A-1H Sky Raiders worked over the airbases runway, fuel reserves, the control tower and hangers. Barracks housing the communist North Vietnamese crews and guards from the base were also bombed by the B-57s. They said there was heavy anti-aircraft fire but none of the aircraft were shot down. The pilots said that when they flew over the base taking pictures they could see that the base was totally destroyed even though they were taking small arms fire as they went across the base. They said the base was about 65 miles north of the 17th parallel and it was an important staging area from which attacks on South Vietnam could be launched. They said that there were many aircraft including communist jets destroyed on the base during the raid. We checked both of the aircraft over real close and found two bullet holes in the tail of 249 but it did little damage.

April 5, 1965

We have been working pretty hard the last couple of days. We had to change the fuel controls on both engines on 243 Monday night. The new ones were no good so we had to change them both again last night. I worked till 4 AM Monday night then till 3 AM Tuesday night. You darn near have to tear the whole engine apart change them. We started at 4 PM Monday night and finished at 4 AM Tuesday morning, and then they have to soak for 12 hours on the airplane, then we have to run the engines to check them out and neither of them checked out. We had to change them a second time. The first time it took us 12 hours to change them but the second time only 9 hours, of course the second time we knew how to do it so we didn't run into so many problems. The second time we changed them they both checked out good.

April 6, 1965

The first American aircraft to be shot down by communist MIGs.

I received a letter from my wife Sheila telling me that two Pilots from her home town (Derby Kansas) had been shot down flying F-105s over North Vietnam.

I checked the local papers and found out North Vietnamese MIG jet fighters pounced from a heavy haze on a formation of U.S. Air Force bombers Sunday and shot down two F-105s. The MIGs were identified as Korean War vintage MIG-15 and 17s then darted away into the haze and escaped apparently unscathed. They carried North Vietnamese markings and were armed with cannon.

The pilots of the 2 F-105's that are among the fastest and most powerful of all American warplanes were lost. One pilot bailed out over the ocean and his drowned body was picked up later. There was no sign of the other pilot or his aircraft after he also headed out to sea. The incident marked the first time Soviet built MIGs have drawn blood from American planes in Vietnam. Both of the F-105s suffered major hits and they both crashed into the sea trying to make it to Da Nang airbase. The MIGs were first sighted over North Vietnam Saturday and several of them made passes at U.S. Navy planes but retreated into the haze before the Navy planes could respond. It was very hazy and they slipped in and hit the two lead planes.

The F-105s were from Mc Connell Air Force Base in Wichita Kansas and both of the pilots lived in Derby where my wife Sheila and her folks live. She later wrote to me again and told me how the little town had reacted.

Viet Cong after ME

April 10, 1965

I was doing the preflight inspection on my aircraft getting it ready for a 6pm takeoff. Major Musgrove came out to the aircraft and said Major Stanfield wanted to see me over at the pilot's operation building. Major Stanfield is not only one of our pilot's; he is also the intelligence officer for our detachment. Since we have this new weapon on our airplanes, the Viet Cong have been pretty mad and they are looking for the pilots and the ground crew. It seems that Major Stanfield got an intelligence report from the South Vietnamese army. The South Vietnamese army had busted a terrorist ring in Saigon after the Embassy bombing and they found a bunch of documents. In those documents they found a picture of my aircraft and a picture of me and my name. They figured it was probably one of the Vietnamese fuel truck drivers that got the information for the Viet Cong. One of the drivers had recently quit and they figured that it was him. Two of our pilot's pictures and names were found, too. This was very disturbing information and Major Stanfield restricted me to the base until further notice. He said if I needed to go to town for any reason to let him know and he would have the Air Police escort me to town to get what I needed and back. I asked him who the pilots were that they had information on but he wouldn't tell me. He said that every since we have the new weapon on our aircraft we have been doing a lot of damage to the Viet Cong and they were after each and every one of us. Two weeks later he called me back and said they decided it would be okay if I went to town during the daytime but I was still restricted from Saigon at night.

More Jets Sent to Vietnam

April 12, 1965

During our now weekly intelligence report at the pilots operation building they reported that an advanced element of a Marine Corps fighter squadron arrived at Da Nang Airbase to add more punch to the growing US Marine task force in the Republic of Vietnam. Four of the new F-4 B Phantom fighters arrived after a five-hour flight.

The 1600 mile an hour jets were led into Da Nang by Lt. Col. William McGraw of St. Louis Missouri, the commander of Marine fighter aircraft squadron 531. The rest of his twin jet tactical fighters were expected Sunday. There are about 18 aircraft in the squadron.

The intelligence report said the phantoms would be used against the North if they are needed. The fighters would come under the operational control of the US Air Force's second air division in Saigon. (They are who we take our orders from on where to send our reconnaissance aircraft). The air division directs US Air Force strikes on North Vietnam, Laos and inside the Republic of Vietnam.

Those of us here in Vietnam were really glad to see the new F-4 Phantoms arriving here in Southeast Asia. The Navy has the F-4B on some of the aircraft carriers in the gulf of Tonkin. The U.S. Air Force has the F-4C now at Clark Air Force Base in the Philippines. Now the Marines have the F-4B at Da Nang Air Base in South Vietnam. That's a lot of F-4 Phantoms all around us and that sure helps us feel maybe a little safer.

Here is some information On the F-4 Phantom from Wikipedia free encyclopedia.

The McDonald Douglas F-4 Phantom is a tandem two seat, twin engine, all weather, long-range supersonic jet fighter /fighter bomber originally developed for the United States Navy. It first entered service in 1960 with the United States Navy. Proving highly adaptable, it was also used by the United States Marine Corps and the US Air Force and by the mid-1960s it had become a major part of their respective air wings.

The Phantom is a large fighter with a top speed of over Mach 2.2. It can carry over 18,000 pounds of weapons on nine external hard points including air to air missiles, air to ground missiles and various bombs. The F-4 like other interceptors of its time was designed without internal cannon. On later models an M 61 Vulcan Rotary Cannon was added to the US Air Force F-4C. Beginning in 1959 it set 15 world records for in-flight performance, including an absolute speed record and an absolute altitude record.

Largest Air Operation of the war to date

April 14, 1965

When I arrived at work at 4pm the day shift guys had 249 and 243 ready for their 6pm takeoffs. Sgt Gogdill told us when the aircraft return from their mission tonight that we need to have all 3 of them ready to fly again for an early morning take off. He said the last flight will be in around 8pm tonight and he will be here to help Chuck Burton and me. He said 237 has had its preflight inspection and is ready to go but will not fly tonight. The day shift will come in early and get all 3 of them in the air for a special mission tomorrow. We are to report back to work around 8am in the morning. When the 3 aircraft return from their morning missions we will need to help the day shift turn them around in 30 minutes and have them ready to fly again. We will need to do this all day long and probably into tomorrow night. He said there is going to be an attack on a large Viet Cong stronghold west of Saigon near the Cambodian border and it will last all day long. Our aircraft and the RF-101s have been taking pictures of the area for the last several days and the Generals running this war have decided to take them out.

They said this was going to be the biggest air raid launched in Indochina since the French fought the communist here and was staged in Tay Ninh Province near the Cambodian border northwest of Saigon.

A U.S. spokesman said American Army, Navy, Air Force and Marine Corps aircraft bombed a communist Viet Cong stronghold from "dawn to dusk". Aircraft from the Aircraft Carrier's Coral Sea and Midway staged their first raid against targets inside the Republic of Vietnam. United

States and Vietnamese Sky Raider bombers also participated in the strike, ordered by General William C Westmoreland several days ago, after Recon reports from our RB-57s. According to U.S. spokesman a total of 230 aircraft dropped 1000 tons of bombs, ranging from 250 pounders to 2000 pounders. The Navy planes dropped the largest bombs. A spokesman said the target area was a jungle region north of the Black forest. It was a maze of blotchy woods with Viet Cong Gardens and numerous trails were visible he said. The target area was about 2 miles wide by 4 miles long. U.S. Air Force and Vietnamese Sky Raiders began the bombing attack at dawn; we have to have one of our aircraft in the air all day long so we have the whole crew working all day and into the night.

Our pilots said ground fire was "surprisingly light considering that it is a dangerous area". The only damage was two Navy planes that received one bullet hole each.

Our Pilots told us U. S. Army armed helicopters flew cover for the Vietnamese aircraft. Marine F-4 Phantoms from Da Nang, Navy F-4 Phantoms from the aircraft carriers in the Gulf of Tonkin and Air Force F-4 Phantoms from Clark Air Force Base in the Philippines also participated in the raid. The raid was directed from the Bien Hoa airbase northeast of Saigon. Our Air Force RB-57 reconnaissance aircraft pictures showed complete destruction of the area.

We worked all day keeping all 3 of our aircraft in the air. They would take off and fly for three hours come back, land, unload the film of the pictures they took, get refueled, and inspected and then back in the air. We had absolutely no problems with any of the aircraft, each one of them came back with no problems at all. At one point when 237 landed the camera guys downloaded the film, we refueled them, inspected the aircraft and they headed back into the air in 15 minutes, "the pilots never even left the cockpit". In total the 3 aircraft flew over 25 hours that day with no mechanical problems. That night Chuck and I sent 249 on a 3 hour flight into North Vietnam and it also came back with no problems. What a fantastic aircraft the B-57 is.

That afternoon 3 F-4 Phantoms from that raid flew over the base in formation, 2 U.S. Air Force F-4Cs and 1 Navy F-4B. When they came in to land the two Air Force Phantoms came in first and made perfectly smooth landings. Then we watched the Navy Phantom coming in really slow it looked like he was going to stall out, he was just hanging in the air and when he hit the runway about 50 feet from the end he slammed it down like he was landing on a carrier. Then he stopped the aircraft at the first turn off and he was up at base operations having coffee before the two Air Force aircraft even come off the end of the other end of the runway. Those Navy pilots were absolutely crazy but they were sure a lot of fun to watch land. I told my friend Chuck Nix, one of the crew Chiefs on one of the RF-101s, that he should run up to base operations and see if he could set up a jet fighter race between his RF- 101 and one of the F-4s. I don't think he ever did, although the RF-101 guys were still hoping that they could get a race with one of those new F-4s.

April 16, 1965

We have just received 8 B- 66 bombers on our crowded flight line. They have been preparing a place for them and have sent almost 200 troops here to take care of them. They are big two engine bombers and have been modified for reconnaissance work. They are quite an aircraft, "all the time broke". It took three weeks for them to get here. They all left Shaw Air Force Base in South Carolina together but ended up strung out half way around the world. Some of them broke down in California, some broke down in Hawaii and some broke down in the Philippines. Every single one of them had problems on their way over here. When the first two of them arrived one of them come in on emergency with engine problems. On the way from Hawaii to Clark AFB one had one engine completely fail and had to land on Wake Island. (I bet that was scary) I sure wish they would go back though. I haven't ever heard anything make so much noise and they are all the time running them. If they have one scheduled to fly they have to get two of them ready, that way they are sure to get at least one of them off the ground if they are lucky. It takes eight man-hours for every hour they fly to keep them in the air. What a piece of junk. I talked to one of their mechanics and he told me that when the aircraft comes back from a mission it will have from 10 to 20 write ups (problems with the aircraft) most of them major problems.

David Karmes

April 18, 1965

I have to be at work at 12 midnight tonight because we have 237 up north and we are not sure when they will return. When I say up north I mean way up north, as far north as you can get without going into China.

I'm afraid that one of these days we are going to lose two pilots and an airplane on these northern missions, they don't just go north but they go north (way north) or otherwise that's way up there where they should not be. I guess they will make it back though, they always do, but I worry about them anyway.

When they returned around 2 am the pilots said it was real hairy for awhile, there were several Chinese MIG jets looking for them. It was a good thing it was night time and they had to fly real low to stay out of the Chinese radar. They said at one point they flew right below a formation of 4 MIGs for almost fifteen minutes until the MIGs turned back north. The MIGs could not see them because they were close below them skimming the treetops. They said they got some good in-frared pictures when they flew over a Chinese air base which means they were no longer in North Vietnam they were in that place that they should not be.

Huge firefight

April 24 1965

What a night, there was a huge fire fight about 5 miles off the east end of the runway. The Viet Cong were attacking a small hamlet east of us. Flares were lighting up the whole sky and HU-1 Huey attack helicopters were firing tracers and red tracer lines were all over the sky. Artillery and mortar explosions were really loud and the A-1H fighter bombers were flying overhead firing rockets from there rocket pods.

It wasn't any big deal to most of us old timers here, we have seen and heard it many times.

We were all standing out on the flight line watching the show when a bunch of the guys from the B-66 bunch come running up to us. They were scared to death and wondering if they should get some weapons and take cover in the sandbag bunkers. It must have taken us an hour to get them calmed down; I thought they were going to go crazy before we convinced them they were perfectly safe. I guess I could understand how they felt because we were the same way when we first got here almost a year ago.

The firefight lasted all night and when I got back to the barracks around midnight some of the new troops were sleeping in the sandbag bunkers we have around the area. I went to bed and slept like a baby.

April 27 1965

We just got word that 245 was over at Clark Air Force Base but it will not be here for a few days because they cannot find the bomb bay door that has the modified camera doors in it. They shipped it from General Dynamics in Texas but they don't know where they shipped it to. They install the fuel ferry tank in the bomb bay of the aircraft so they can make it across the Pacific Ocean and it has a different bomb bay door. They have all the other equipment installed but they need that door.

CHAPTER 12

MAY 1965

Saturday May 1, 1965

Today is my first day on the day shift and I do not like it at all, it is way too hot here on the flight line in the daytime. The reason I am on days now is because I only have one month left and we have plenty of help now. Sgt. Cogdill said I am no longer assigned as the crew chief on 249 and if I need to take a day or two off just let him know so he won't worry about me. I told him that I would just as soon work because it makes the time go faster but I may occasionally be late for work until I get used to getting up early in the morning. Matter of fact I was an hour late this morning my first day then about 4pm at quitting time we were all setting around in the office and Sgt. Gogdill said "by the way Dave you weren't supposed to start days until Monday". Then he said go ahead and go to dinner at the chow hall then get back down here and help Burton and a couple of the new guys "you have 2 flights tonight". Everybody thought that was really funny and were busting a gut laughing and I did help Chuck that night.

245 Returns from General Dynamics

About 2pm that afternoon we were changing the L/H engine starter on 243 when one of the guys said "look up", just then here came this beautiful black RB-57 right over our heads flying right down the flight line past the control tower then pulled up turned around and came in and landed.

Our 245 was home and wow did it ever look good. We had quite a crowd come out to see it, even the base commander showed up. We refueled the aircraft and inspected it real close and everything looked good, the pilot said everything was working great and there were no problems.

It has all the new camera upgrades including a closed circuit TV system including a zoom lens. That's so they can fly along and see in real time what is under them and call an air strike without having to land and develop the films. The camera is in the bomb bay and the TV is in the back cockpit along with all the new scopes and the new terrain following radar system.

The aircraft really looks good painted black with red letters and markings on it.

The engines haven't even cooled and the armament guys are already reinstalling the new weapon on the aircraft. We sure have been cleaning up on the Viet Cong with that thing. Of course they are getting wise to it now and they take cover whenever we fly over now. I guess the Viet Cong were still after me but I wasn't really worried about them, I stay on the base most of the time anyway, especially at night.

That night after dinner I went back down to the flight line to help Chuck Burton for when the aircraft returned even though I didn't have to. Chuck and his crew already had the aircraft in the air and I noticed that 245 was not there. Chuck said the pilots (I think it was Major Musgrove but it might have been one of the new pilots as in my letter I did not name them) had come out on the flight line and said they wanted to fly 245 instead of 249 which had been scheduled, he wanted to check out the new equipment. So Chuck and his crew got 245 ready and 237 for Major Stanfield and Lt. Platt.

When 237 returned around 8pm Major Stanfield said the only problem with 237 was the light was out for the altimeter. He said to holler at them over at the operations building when 245 returned. They had called them and said they had used the closed circuit TV system and they would be a little late. They were going to hang around and get some Photo Flash pictures of the strike they had just called in.

When they returned around 9pm everybody that was over at operations came out to meet them to see what had happened. When they taxied in and stopped the pilot said everything was working great on the aircraft and he told the camera guys to let him know as soon as they developed the pictures and Chuck told them also to let him know as we want to see them also.

Puff the Magic Dragon

They said they were working on their target area and they could see many camp fires in the jungle below them using the new closed circuit TV system. There was a large concentration of Viet Cong or maybe North Vietnamese troops below them. They called in and reported what they were seeing and was told a strike would be coming from Bien Hoa air base.

They were told that one of the new Douglas AC-47 gunships was in the air patrolling around the base and they have been diverted to your area and would be there soon. We have heard rumors that the guys up at Bien Hoa airbase had converted a couple of C-47 cargo aircraft by installing fast firing Gatling Guns in it. They call it "Puff the Magic Dragon".

The pilots said when the AC-47 showed up they climbed up and circled the area to watch the show and get some pictures. The first thing the AC-47 did was drop some flares that lit up the whole area. Then they put the AC-47 in a steep bank to the left and circled the area they wanted to fire on. Then they opened fire with 3 fast firing Gatling Guns coming out of the left side of the aircraft. The pilots said it was amazing watching the red tracers and the amount of fire power coming out of that old cargo plane. A few minutes later when the AC-47 was done they went in and got some pictures.

Later that night the camera guys brought over a couple of the photos. They showed several trucks on fire and supply storage areas burning and many bodies all over the place. Everything was destroyed and the pictures showed it was an extremely large contingent of North Vietnamese troops. I guess 245s first day home showed that all that new equipment is well worth the price.

Here is some information from Wikipedia free encyclopedia on the Douglas AC-47 Spooky (also nicknamed "Puff the Magic Dragon")

The Douglas AC-47 was the first in a series of gunships developed by the United States Air Force during the Vietnam War. More firepower than could be provided by light and medium ground- attack aircraft was thought to be needed in some situations when ground forces called for close air support.

The AC-47 was a United States Air Force C-47 cargo aircraft, the military version of the Douglas DC-3 that had been modified by mounting three 7.62 mm General Electric miniguns to fire through two rear window openings and the side cargo door, all on the pilots left side of the aircraft. The modified aircrafts primary function was close air support for ground troops. The guns were actuated by a control on the pilot's yoke whereby he could control the guns either individually or together, although gunners were also among the crew to assist with gun failures and similar issues. It could orbit the target for hours, providing suppressing fire over an elliptical area approximately 52 yards in diameter, placing a round every 2.4 yards during a 3 second burst. The aircraft also could drop flares to illuminate the battleground.

The AC-47 had no previous design to gauge how successful it would be because it was the first of its kind. In 1964 Capt. Ron W Terry returned from temporary duty in Vietnam as part of an Air Force Systems Command team reviewing all aspects of air operations and counter-insurgency warfare. Where he had noted the usefulness of C-47's and C-123's orbiting as flare ships during night attacks on fortified hamlets. He received permission to conduct a live fire test using the C-47 and he conceived the side firing gunship program.

Capt. Terry and a testing team arrived at Bien Hoa Airbase, South Vietnam on 2 December 1964, with equipment needed to modify 2 C-47s. The first test aircraft a C 47B mail courier converted to C 47D was ready by December 11, the second by December 15, 1964 and both were allocated to the first Air Commando Squadron at Bien Hoa Airbase for combat testing. The newly dubbed AC 47 often operated under the radio call sign "Puff". Its primary mission involved protecting villages, hamlets, and personnel from massive attacks by Viet Cong guerrilla units. The aircraft was nick named "Puff the Magic Dragon" because of the "Puff" radio call sign plus when those 3 mini-guns start firing they sound like a dragon coming at you from the ground.

The early gunship trials were so successful, the second aircraft was returned to the United States early in 1965 to provide crew training. In July 1965 headquarters USAF ordered Tactical Air Command to establish an AC-47 squadron. Now using the call sign "Spooky" each of its three 7.62 mm mini-guns could selectively fire either 50 or 100 rounds per second. Cruising in an overhead left-hand orbit at 120 knots airspeed and an altitude of 3000 feet the gunship could put a bullet or glowing red tracer (every fifth round) into every square yard of a football field sized target and potentially in less than 10 seconds. And as long as it's 45 flare and 24,000 rounds basic load of ammunition held out they could do this intermittently while loitering over the target for hours.

After reading that information on the AC-47 gun ship and remembering those pictures that 245 took, now I understand why there was so much destruction on those pictures.

245 a very Special Aircraft

To those of us that worked on the early Patricia Lynn Project 245 was the most special aircraft. Although 243 was special also, 245 was the first to be painted black and it looked so good. We loved those two aircraft and we took care of them like they were our children. We fixed them when they broke and bandaged them up when they were many times wounded. They never lacked for anything as we had top priority on the base and we received whatever we asked for. We had the best Commander in all of the United States Air Force "Major Musgrove" and the best maintenance Boss in the Air Force "Sgt Gogdill". Not to say we didn't love 237 and 249 they were great aircraft also but 245 is special. Most of the later pictures you see of the Patricia Lynn RB-57E are of aircraft Serial number 55-4245. My new friends over in Great Briton, that are modelers, desire her as one of their favorite models to build, the RB-57E Patricia Lynn Serial number 55-4245 from the Vietnam War. I have been kicking around the idea of maybe building one myself, we will see maybe later.

245 on the ramp before it was painted black

There were seven B-57E aircraft modified by General Dynamics at Fort Worth, Texas into RB-57E all weather recon aircraft. The first two aircraft 55-4243 and 55-4245 when completed were assigned to the 405th Fighter wing at Clark Air force Base in the Philippines then to Detachment 1 of the 33rd Camron at Tan Son Nhut Airfield, Saigon South Vietnam in May of 1963. There was also a 55-4244 that was kept at General Dynamics to train the air crews. Then in January of 1965 two more aircraft were completed 55-4237 and 55-4249 and they arrived in South Vietnam that same month. Later that year in December 55-4264 was completed and sent to Vietnam. One more aircraft was modified to replace the two aircraft that were shot down, 243 was lost in August of 1965 and 264 in December 1968.

After the war in Vietnam, from what I can find out, the remaining 5 were destroyed and cut up for scrap. What a shame that at least one of these important aircraft could not of have been saved in a Museum somewhere. Although I never did find out the serial number of the last aircraft that was modified maybe there is hope yet that one could have survived.

David Karmes

Russian Surface to Air Missile sites (SAM)

May 10, 1965

Most of our flights are going into North Vietnam lately, we have been monitoring what the pilots say are the Russians building surface to air missile (SAM) sites around Hanoi. Our pilots tell us they have been monitoring the construction of these sites for several weeks. They say they cannot understand why the people running this war are not destroying them before they are completed. They figure they don't want to upset the Russians, but if they complete them we definitely will lose some aircraft and crews.

Things seem to be really heating up around here also and there is a lot of Viet Cong activity close to the base here. There has been mortar and artillery fire all night and all day today. It is about 6 or 7 miles away though and the new troops are still pretty nervous but they will get used to it. There are many new troops being sent to Vietnam including 15,000 U.S. Marines around Da Nang up north. I sure am glad to see the U. S. troop and equipment build up but I am glad I will be out of here in a few weeks.

Things are also heating up all over South Vietnam; U.S. jets flew 58 sorties against suspected Viet Cong positions and concentrations inside the Republic of Vietnam.

The biggest single strike was by 16 Marine F-4B Phantoms in Quang Nam province where the key American airbase at Da Nang is located. Our pilots told us they took pictures of the battle damage from this operation plus pictures of a new base the Marines are building south of Da Nang.

Here is a report we received at our weekly intelligence briefing.

US Marines established a beachhead on a desolate coastal plain 52 miles South East of Da Nang Friday and launched immediately into their first mission, building a 4000 foot airstrip to be used for air operations in central Vietnam.

The airstrip will have an aluminum runway base with catapults and arresting gear similar to that used on aircraft carriers. It will be capable of handling most types of aircraft including Marine and Navy F-4 B Phantom jets. The US Seabees that came ashore Friday estimated the job could be done in 72 hours once all the equipment had been unloaded from ships anchored off the beach. Friday's Marine landing brings the total of Marines in Vietnam to 15,000; it was the fourth Marine landing this year.

Friday's landing was described by the commander of the task force Rear Adm. Donald Wilson as the largest amphibious landing in the Far East since the Inchon Korea landing in 1950. The landing was completed in 13 minutes and was made in perfect weather.

When the Marines landed they didn't even get their feet wet. Waiting on the sand was a group of high-ranking officers who had arrived moments before by helicopter. The more F-4 Phantoms we can get over here the better I like it.

Disaster at Bien Hoa Airbase

Sunday May 16 1965

Sgt. Cogdill came over to the barracks about 10am and rounded up all of the RB-57 crew that he could find. He said that there had been an incident at Bien Hoa Airbase and 7 armed B-57Bs were coming in to Tan Son Nhut and we have to take care of them.

Bien Hoa Airbase is about 20 miles from Saigon and Sunday morning at about 8:30 AM a Navy F-8 Crusader jet fighter landed there on emergency. They parked him down in the jet parking ramp where 11 B-57Bs were all loaded with 500 pound bombs and napalm bombs ready to go out on a strike against the Viet-Cong. The F-8s guns were loaded, so they sent a crew out to disarm them. While they were disarming him one of his 20 mm cannons went off and hit a napalm bomb hanging on a B-57 that was just ready to taxi out to the runway. When the fireworks ended there were 11 B- 57s completely destroyed along with several A1 H's and A-1Es plus other aircraft. They haven't got a complete count on the dead or injured people yet; last count was 29 dead and 60 or more injured. They expect the dead to come to around 50 people. It happened right when the maintenance people were doing their before flight inspections on their airplanes and the ramp was full of all kinds of people. There were 5 B- 57s that had just taxied out and were at the end of the runway ready to take off. Two more were already in the air.

The pilots and ground crew hardly knew what hit them. I have guys I know up there working on the B- 57's. I don't know how many of them were killed as I haven't seen a casualty list yet. We heard that only three people that were on the flight line got out alive. They say that the ramp was completely leveled in 2 minutes. Some of the pilots that were strapped in their seats with engines running literally ejected out of the aircraft while they were sitting on the ground to escape the fires.

As of now there are only 7 B- 57B's in this country not counting our RB- 57's so they all had to land here at Ton Son Nhut. They are going to operate out of here with three combat missions per day and you can guess who was going to have to take care of them, us! They are sending all the troops that are still alive down here to help but they don't number very many. Just the few that worked night shift at Bien Hoa. So you can see that we are going to be pretty busy for the next week or so. They are only supposed to stay until they get the base at Bien Hoa cleaned up.

We will fly three missions with each of those seven aircraft per day plus take care of our own aircraft. They say they are sending some more troops from Clark Air Force Base over here to help take care of them and we plan on running 16 hour shifts starting on Monday. I'm not too crazy about working around those armed aircraft, they seem to be jinxed. But we have to do it; the war has to go on.

On the official report a spokesman said a chain reaction of explosions destroyed every B- 57 Canberra bomber parked on the base flight line. Of the rest of Bien Hoa's 18 Canberra's, seven were spared because they had already taken off on morning missions or were at the opposite end of the runway preparing to take off. Those planes will have to move to Tan Son Nhut Airfield in Saigon and be maintained by the RB-57 maintenance crews that are already there.

The fires along the parking ramp forced the abandonment of the nearby base command post and tactical operations center. The flames were still out of control at midmorning spreading toward an ammunition dump. An American transport plane flying over the base reported that the entire flight line was "wiped out". The pilot reported that columns of black smoke were billowing thousands of feet into the air.

Seven minutes after the first explosion, the base reported that seven bombs have exploded on the ramp, and jet fuel had been set afire. The blasts and flames leapt to another parking line, where two propeller driven aircraft were reported ablaze. Bien Hoa is one of the bases from which American aircraft bomb communist North Vietnam.

I remember when a Communist mortar barrage thundered into the base before dawn last November 1, 1964 destroying or damaging a score of the B- 57 Canberra's. That raid killed four Americans and two Vietnamese and wounded 72 servicemen. The communist success helped lead to the stationing of the 173rd airborne brigade in Vietnam for the protection of Bien Hoe and another base 40 miles Southeast of Saigon.

That mortar bombardment caused a similar chain reaction among the parked bombers leading to some criticism over previous failure to separate the Jets by sandbag barriers. A spokesman said later that construction of such barriers was going on around the clock. Newsman who visited the base before the accident noticed that the B-57s were still parked wingtip to wingtip with no intervening barriers.

The next day an American military spokesman said 26 Americans and Vietnamese were dead and 100 wounded in the aftermath of the disaster which hit the airbase early Sunday morning. The spokesman said that two of the 22 hospitalized wounded are listed in serious condition. The whole ramp area where the jet planes are parked was a mass of debris. Pieces of wings and fuselage were scattered over the flight line at the airbase.

US paratroopers securing the base immediately went on alert and patrols were sent beyond the base perimeter to prevent the Viet Cong from capitalizing on the situation. The Defense Department is sending an investigative team from Washington to Bien Hoa Airbase headed by Lt. General William Martin, Air Force inspector general.

Twenty two planes were destroyed and eighteen damaged. The aircraft losses suffered Sunday represented 10% of America's worldwide nuclear capable B- 57 fleet said Maj. Gen. Joseph H Moore, Commander of U.S. Air Force Second Air Division. He stressed that the loss would have a "negligible effect" on American Air Force operations in Vietnam and replacement aircraft could be in Vietnam in a matter of hours. But regarding the use of the base at Bien Hoa he said it would be a week before it would be operative. Officials estimated the cost of destruction will exceed $20 million.

In addition to the destruction of the aircraft, the concussion from the blast knocked out the Bien Hoa control tower, collapsed the walls of hangers and caused other damage. Officials said the deaths and damage of Sunday's disaster far exceeded such American disasters as the US Embassy bombing, the mortar attack on Bien Hoa last November and the Pleiku army barracks shelling.

Armed B-57Bs Arrive at Ton Son Nhut

Monday May17, 1965

All seven of the aircraft from Bien Hoa are here now and we sure did work our butts off all day today, we went to work at 7 AM and got off at 7 PM. We flew 2 combat missions each with 4 airplanes, one this morning and one this afternoon. When we got to work the armament people had the bombs and guns loaded already but when they got back from their first mission we had to help load the bombs and the guns. Those armed aircraft sure make me nervous after what happened at Bien Hoa.

Those guys they sent down here from Bien Hoa aren't much help either, they walk around in a daze most of the time. But I guess I would too if I had seen more than half my friends and the guys I work with killed. Can't really blame them though, but they sure aren't much help.

Wow is it ever raining hard this afternoon; this is the first hard rain we have had in 3 days. I am glad to see it though because when it rains like this I did not think I would have to be around those armed B-57s; I was wrong we sent them off anyway. You may think "I'm chicken", if you do you are right (I am chicken). I don't want any part of them and I am going to stay away from them as much as possible. Besides I don't have enough time left here to be brave. The guys kid me about every time I walk in front of one of those guns I duck under them. They can get their heads blown off if they want to, because those guns are libel to go off any time if there is any static electricity running around in the airplane.

I thought our pilots that fly the RB-57s were the bravest but they don't hold a candle to these guys that fly these armed B-57s. It was raining so hard you could not see 20 feet in front of you and these guys somehow taxied out to the runway and took off because someone was under attack. We sat in the truck and watched them take off, actually we could not see them because it was raining so hard but we could hear them and I know they could not see the runway. I wonder if there is such a thing as an instrument takeoff.

Going Home

Friday May 19 1965

I arrived at work at 7am to help fly 10 missions today of the armed B-57s. When I got there Captain Chrisman called me on the phone from the orderly room. He told me I have a confirmed seat on the 28th of May to go home. I will be leaving one week early and I don't have to worry about being bumped off, it is confirmed I will be leaving on a Pan American Boeing 707 on Friday the 28th of May. Wow! Was I ever glad to hear that, I can hardly wait to get home to my beautiful wife that I have missed so dearly. It's about a 20 hour flight including ground time. I get my amended booking orders tomorrow morning and tomorrow is my last day at work. One more day with those darn "HOT" B-57s and I will be through with them. That's one day too many though, those things sure do make me nervous.

Tuesday May 23 1965

I started clearing the base today, turned in my tool box, turned in all my field gear that I never did use which included my back pack, helmet, my pistol and gun belt, my ammunition, canteen and first aid kit. Then I had to get a bunch of shots over at the health clinic. I didn't like it but I did it anyway because they wouldn't let me leave without them. I did it all in one day then spent the next 4 days just goofing off down on the flight line. Watched the guys work, played a little horseshoes, drank a little beer and lay around on the sandbags watching the aircraft land and takeoff and said goodbye to the great friends I had made.

Friday May 28 1965

That morning at 6am I boarded that beautiful Pan American Boeing 707 (that have real beautiful American women to take care of us) and when we left that runway at Tan Son Nuut airfield Saigon, South Vietnam everyone on that aircraft was clapping and hollering and not a one of us looked back.

My ride home Boeing 707

We headed out over the South China Sea headed for Clark Air Force Base in the Philippines where we landed to pick up some more troops. Then off we went toward home and we landed on every rock that sticks out of the Pacific Ocean. First up was Wake Island where we picked up 2 more troops on their way home. It took us two attempts to takeoff of that rock with its short runway. That was kind of scary when the pilots brought us to a screeching halt when we were halfway down the runway on takeoff then turned around taxied back to the end of the runway and tried it again, we made it on the second try thank God. Next up was Guam Island where we picked up a couple more people and had no problem taking off there; thankfully they have a longer runway. The next stop was Honolulu International airport Hawaii. There they let us get off the airplane while they refueled and serviced everything. When we got off the airplane most of the guys kissed the beautiful United States ground including me. From Hawaii we took off for the Mainland U.S.A. where we landed at Travis Air force Base at San Francisco, California "we were home".

The only problem was it was Memorial Day weekend and no one was there to discharge me from the United States Air Force, I had to wait until Tuesday.

Tuesday morning we did all the paperwork and by 2pm that afternoon I was no longer a member of the United States Air Force. Then I ran into another problem, I could not get a flight out of San Francisco until the next day to Wichita, Kansas where my beautiful wife was waiting. But I could get a flight out to Oklahoma City that evening. So I called Sheila and they agreed to pick me up there which is about a 2 hour drive from Wichita.

When I got off that airplane my beautiful wife Sheila ran into my arms and I was HOME!

Now here I am 71 years old 50 years later reliving Vietnam through these letters.

I do want to say my year in Vietnam may not have been typical to other Vietnam Veterans unless maybe they were there during the early years of the war. I have the utmost admiration for my brothers that were combat solders. And to those that lost loved ones in the Vietnam War I feel I can say for those of us that served we miss them also.

Sheila and I will celebrate our 52nd wedding anniversary on Dec 15 2014 with 4 beautiful College educated children, 2 boys and 2 girls, 6 beautiful Grand Children and 3 Great Grand Children with more to come. GOD IS GREAT dave@karmes.com

Made in the USA
Coppell, TX
27 November 2019